Paul Hollywood's
BREAD

Paul Hollywood's
BREAD

How to make great breads into even greater meals

Photography by Peter Cassidy

BLOOMSBURY

LONDON · NEW DELHI · NEW YORK · SYDNEY

To Alexandra and Josh, and the rest of my baking family.

First published in Great Britain 2013

Text © 2013 Love Productions Ltd and Paul Hollywood
Photography © 2013 Peter Cassidy

By arrangement with the BBC. The BBC is a trademark of the British Broadcasting Corporation
and is used under licence. BBC logo © BBC 1996.

The moral right of the author has been asserted.

Bloomsbury Publishing Plc, 50 Bedford Square, London WC1B 3DP
Bloomsbury Publishing, London, New Delhi, New York and Sydney
www.bloomsbury.com
A CIP catalogue record for this book is available from the British Library.

ISBN 978 14088 4069 6
10 9 8 7 6 5 4 3 2 1

PROJECT EDITOR Janet Illsley
DESIGNERS Peter Dawson, Louise Evans www.gradedesign.com
PHOTOGRAPHER Peter Cassidy
FOOD EDITOR Hattie Ellis
HOME ECONOMIST Lizzie Harris
PROPS STYLIST Róisín Nield
INDEXER Hilary Bird

Printed and bound by Mohn Media, Germany

Innovative use of combined heat and
power technology when printing this
product reduced CO$_2$ emissions
by up to 52% in comparison to
conventional methods in Germany.

Note

My baking times in the recipes are for fan-assisted ovens. If you are using a conventional
oven, you will need to increase the oven setting by around 10–15°C. Ovens vary, so use
an oven thermometer to verify the temperature and check your bread towards the end
of the suggested cooking time.

It is time to take bread off the side plate and put it back where it belongs: in the centre of the table. My book has two aims. First of all I want to teach you how to bake a wide variety of breads. And then I want to show how versatile bread is. Each of the breads in this book has a 'spin off' dish – starter, salad, main course or dessert – that the loaf is very much part of. So this is more than a baking book: it's about the whole meal.

Perhaps because bread is everywhere, people forget how it can be the key food on the table. In the Mediterranean, where I lived for six years on the island of Cyprus, bread is the focal point of family eating, with everyone leisurely sitting around the table, chewing on bread with some pâté and salad, and talking together. To me, that's what 'breaking bread' is about: coming together, tucking in, nourishment and pleasure.

The most successful dinner party I've had was after I had baked a batch of sourdough baguettes at work one morning. I brought them home, put them on the table that evening, opened some red wine and served apples, cheese, wine and pâté with the bread. Everyone left saying it was the most enjoyable meal they'd ever had. So when I'm presented with an anaemic roll on a side plate in a restaurant, well, that's when I get wound up.

I learnt to bake as a teenager, picking up skills and knowledge by working in my Dad's chain of bakeries. I moved on to become head baker at The Chester Grosvenor for five years, and after that at The Dorchester and Cliveden hotels. Then I went abroad and lived in Cyprus, learning how to bake Mediterranean-style breads and passing on what I knew about baking. Six years later I came back to Britain, started my own bakery, became involved in television and everything took off. *The Great British Bake Off* was a runaway success. Viewers in their millions were switched on to bread, cakes, pastry and pies, and turning on their ovens.

I'm proud to be a part of the revolution in baking in this country. People are making their own loaves, trying each other's, and buying bread from proper bakeries. Shops are selling different kinds of flour and baking equipment. Cooks used to be more scared of making a loaf of bread than a Victoria sponge, but once you've got the techniques right, it's even more fulfilling. A cake has its place: afternoon tea. Bread can be put on the table at breakfast, lunch, tea and supper. This book shows you how.

Bread baking is the easiest thing to learn – just a few very simple ingredients put together – and the hardest to master. But I'm going to take you through the techniques, passing on my secrets and giving you plenty of tips on how to bake. I'll be guiding you with step-by-step instructions and photographs so you have the confidence and ability to make each bread.

Prehistoric man kneaded dough. Baking is in our psyche, but one crucial ingredient you need for success is passion. If you have that, then you'll want to better yourself. Nobody will be more critical about your bakes than you. Put in the time and effort, notice what happens in each bake, keep learning and everyone will enjoy what you do – not least you. One of the secrets to being a good baker is understanding consistency: what the dough should feel like. It's a touch thing, and you'll have more and more knowledge at your fingertips the more you practise.

Be warned: many people find that baking is addictive. Once you get into it, you just want to bake more and more. It's not just about wanting to get better. There's also something magical about the transformative nature of baking. You start off with a slop in a bowl and end up with something crisp, warm and full of flavour that goes with anything.

Beyond this, you turn a house into a home when you fill it with bread. Everyone wants to be around a place that smells of baking. Once you've put that knife into your loaf and heard the crust splinter, then you get the wonderful smell of the crumb. By the time you've given a slice to your mother, partner, kids, friends, neighbours, aunties, there's nothing left.

With these bread recipes and their spin-off dishes, you'll turn simple ingredients into some of the best meals you've ever eaten.

EQUIPMENT

Bread doesn't need much kit: a bowl, a baking tray and an oven are the main requirements. Here are the most useful basic tools of the trade.

Measuring equipment
Digital scales make it easy to weigh small amounts, and a set of accurate measuring spoons is essential.

Baker's scraper
This is a useful tool for dividing the dough (into rolls, for example) and to clean down your work surface so that the dough doesn't stick.

The best scrapers are those with a solid metal blade and a plastic or metal handle; you can also buy plastic ones. Your scraper should be solid enough so the blade can cut through the dough and not bend.

Plastic tubs
I like to use oiled plastic boxes to contain wetter doughs as they rise, because it helps keep their shape. This is particularly true of ciabatta, as you want to keep the dough light and airy before baking.

Bannetons
Bannetons are baskets that can be used to prove loaves. Traditionally made of wicker and round or long in shape, they are sometimes also lined with linen to prevent sticking. They are especially useful for wetter loaves, such as sourdoughs, to keep the shape and lift. A standard bowl can be used instead.

Tins and baking trays
Buy non-stick Teflon-coated tins and sturdy non-stick baking trays. The most useful loaf tin to have is a 1kg tin (about 27 x 14 x 7.5cm). As an alternative you can season standard tins and trays to make them non-stick: brush the surface with a little lard or oil, put it into a hot oven for about an hour, then turn off the oven and leave inside overnight with the door closed. Never wash your seasoned tin – just wipe it down with a warm cloth so you don't scrape the surface. What you are doing is building up a resistance to the dough sticking. The more you use your seasoned tin or tray, the less it will stick. Otherwise, line with baking parchment (not greaseproof) or silicone paper.

Pastry brush, rolling pin and bowls
These are all useful bits of kit you'll have in your kitchen anyway. I prefer rolling pins that have a handle on the same level as the pin. Pastry brushes are useful for getting glazes evenly onto breads. Use big, roomy bowls for rising bread, so it can expand well without flowing over.

INGREDIENTS

Bread is made from four main ingredients: flour, yeast, salt and water. You can have those in your house all the time and make bread whenever you want.

Flour

To make bread you need 'strong' flour. This is flour with the high level of protein – in the form of gluten – needed to give your bread its stretch and strength and a good chewy crumb. It's important to remember that different types of flour have different protein levels and so do different brands of the same kind of flour. This will determine how much liquid the flour will absorb and may slightly affect your recipe. When making a new loaf, find a brand of flour you like and stick to it, especially when you are learning to bake, so you get used to how it works. It's a bit like when you are starting to drive – changing the car throws you slightly.

STRONG WHITE FLOUR

White flour has the highest protein level of all the strong flours (12% and over) and this makes it easy to get a good rise and light bread. You can also add some strong white flour to other flours with less protein to help them lift and hold. Bakers buy the best quality, highest protein flour they can because they get more volume in the loaf and a better bake.

PLAIN AND SELF-RAISING WHITE FLOUR

Plain flour is used for cakes, biscuits and pastry, as well as soda bread. You get a more crumbly texture with plain flour, with its lower protein level (9–11%), but you need to be sure you don't overwork doughs with plain flour or they can become tough.

Self-raising flour contains baking powder and needs no other raising agent. It is mainly used for cakes.

STRONG WHOLEMEAL FLOUR

This is one of my favourite flours because it has so much flavour, especially when it's stoneground. I sometimes mix wholemeal with other flours to get a more complex loaf and add strong white flour to get more lift. Wholemeal flour absorbs more water than white and requires a slightly longer knead.

MALTED FLOUR

Malted flour is slightly darker in colour than white flour because of the addition of tasty malted wheat flakes. You also see it sold as 'Granary' flour. Brands differ slightly in their composition, so it is worth trying several to see which one you like best.

RYE FLOUR

Rye is a grass that is different to wheat and has less gluten. Much used in German and Scandinavian baking, it is making a comeback here as well. The flour is slightly more difficult to work with than other flours because it is low in protein (below 10%) and makes a heavy dough that takes longer to rise, but it is worth using in a mix with other flours.

SPELT FLOUR

Known as a 'grandfather grain', spelt is an ancestor of modern wheat that has been rediscovered. With less gluten than its descendants, it is best combined with other stronger flours and baked in a tin to give the dough a bit of a rise. There's been some publicity advocating spelt as a healthy grain that can be eaten by those who are gluten-intolerant, but it does still contain some gluten.

Yeast

If you're going to bake, you've got to understand the beast that is yeast. This micro-organism needs feeding and looking after. If you put it in the wrong environment, it won't work so well. But treat it right and it'll give you something you really want to eat.

These days, I always use fast-action dried yeast, also called instant yeast. It contains ascorbic acid (vitamin C), which helps the rising action. I find it more convenient than fresh yeast, which doesn't keep for long, and ordinary dried yeast, which needs rehydrating in warm water and is trickier to use.

Once you've been baking for a while, you can start to play around with yeast levels. The slower the rise, the more flavour your dough acquires, and adding less yeast is one way of slowing down the rise. For my recipes, you should stick to the same quantities of flour and water, but after a while you could try lowering the yeast to get different results.

Salt

Salt levels are a personal taste. I'd suggest a minimum of 7g per 500g of flour and a maximum, if you really like salt, of 11–12g per 500g of flour. On the whole, 7–10g is best. It also depends what you are serving with your bread. The Tuscans, for example, put no salt at all in their bread but the rest of their diet has plenty of cured meats and fish.

My bread recipes use ordinary cooking salt. If you want to use sea salt, then use the fine-grained kind.

When adding salt to the dry ingredients, put it on the other side of the bowl to the yeast. Salt will slow down (and even kill) the yeast in its concentrated form so it's a good habit to add them separately. You can also dissolve the salt in the water and add it that way to disperse it well throughout the dough.

Water

The quantity of water in a dough makes a difference to how much it rises and the structure of the crumb. Novice bakers tend to make their dough too dry.

As a general rule, it's better to add the water to the flour in stages. A cheap, lower protein flour will take less water than a high-quality one. Add about three-quarters of the water to start with and then slowly add as much as you can of the rest until you get a soft dough. The more experienced you become, the more water you'll be able to add as you get better at kneading and handling wetter doughs.

Some recipes recommend adding warm water to a dough to get the yeast working. I tend to use tap-cool water because I prefer a slower rise that gives more flavour to the bread. The one exception is sourdough, because the yeasts in the starter can do with a little help; there's already plenty of flavour in the mixture and sourdough always has a long, slow rise. In this case use tepid or lukewarm water; if the water is too hot it will kill the yeast.

You can use liquids other than water in your dough – cider and beer are two good ones to try – but be aware that they can affect the way the yeast functions. Milk is mildly acidic and will slow the yeast up, as will adding egg to your dough.

Bicarbonate of soda and baking powder

Bicarbonate of soda is an alkaline powder that reacts when it comes into contact with an acid and liquid, such as buttermilk, to produce carbon dioxide that makes bread rise. It works more quickly than yeast but, if you have time, it's still worth giving the dough a rest of 15–30 minutes before baking, to allow the soda time to start working.

Baking powder contains both an acid and an alkaline, which only react once liquid is added. Doughs containing baking powder should be baked straight away.

Fats

The addition of fat to a dough – typically butter or olive oil – helps to soften our bread and improves its keeping quality. I use unsalted butter in my Stilton and bacon rolls and malt loaf, but for most breads I prefer olive oil.

Flavourings

You can add extra ingredients to bread dough to flavour it but you do need to think about how that will affect the chemistry of your bread. Onion, for example, is an acid and you need to be careful about how much you add or the yeast won't work so well. In my experience, subtle rather than strong flavours come through best in bread.

TECHNIQUES

Mixing
Combining the dry and liquid ingredients to make a dough

This simple start to making bread needs some care. Different flours absorb different amounts of liquid and you want to add it gradually to get the right amount. People tend to add too little water at this mixing stage because a wetter dough is initially harder to work with and makes your hands messy. But more moisture makes a better loaf and you get better at working with wet doughs with experience.

You're not kneading at this point but using one hand like a claw (see photograph, right) to scrunch the ingredients together and to get a feel for how the flour is absorbing the liquid. When all the flour comes away from the side of the bowl, and you've got a good soft dough, the job's done.

One other important mixing tip is to add the yeast and salt to different sides of the bowl. In its concentrated form, salt will slow down or kill the yeast, so these two vital ingredients are best kept apart.

Kneading
Developing the gluten in the dough to give it stretch and strength

Kneading works the gluten in the flour thoroughly and is essential for getting an elastic dough that will rise and hold the air as it proves and bakes.

Everyone has their own way of kneading. Mine works for me and you can follow it first and develop your own method. I stretch the dough out, fold it into the centre, flatten it – bang, bang, bang – and turn it. Keep repeating this: stretch, fold, flatten, turn. You've got to work the dough through its stickiness and over time you'll feel it getting smoother and stretchier. Put lots of energy into the task: it's a proper workout!

I tend to use oil, rather than flour, on the work surface to stop the dough sticking so much, and you can also use a baker's scraper to clean up the dough as you knead. If you do dust the surface with flour, don't use too much or you will throw out your recipe and tighten the dough. I also use flour when the dough contains butter or eggs, as the saturated fat would react adversely with oil.

Most beginners don't knead for long enough. Once you get experienced, you'll be a bit quicker, but most people should knead their dough for at least 10 minutes. The better the elastic gluten you develop now, the stronger the rise and hold will be in your end loaf. To test when you've kneaded enough, tease and pull out a piece of the dough between your hands: it should be able to stretch about 20cm without breaking.

Rising
Producing carbon dioxide that makes the dough rise, and developing flavour

Now let nature do the work. Put the dough in a roomy, lightly oiled bowl, to stop it sticking, and cover the bowl with a clean tea towel or cling film to protect the dough from draughts and to stop a skin forming on the dough and slowing the rise. I don't recommend putting rising dough in an especially warm place in an attempt to speed things up, because a slower rise gives more flavour to the bread. Most houses with central heating are warm enough, even in the depths of winter. There's no need to put the bowl in an airing cupboard or on a shelf over a radiator. Anywhere in the kitchen should be fine.

The yeast feeds on the nutrients in the flour and produces the carbon dioxide that makes the dough rise. You'll know that you are harnessing the yeasty power because you will be able to smell the dough fermenting.

Leave the dough until it at least doubles in size – it may treble or even quadruple. If you can, let it grow to its full extent, when you'll see creases just starting to form on the top. Don't leave your dough any longer though, or it will over-ferment and the bread may taste bitter.

Knocking back
Pushing down the air pockets and tightening the dough

Knocking back deflates the dough by taking out the air pockets, which is important to create a uniform texture that allows the dough to rise again evenly. Knock the risen dough down and work it a bit so the yeast gets going again. Push it down properly – use the strength in the heels of your hands, your knuckles and then your fingertips.

It is critical that you then fold your dough in on itself several times to give it structure. This is like folding paper. Fold paper once and it's flimsy. Fold it several times and it's a more cohesive, compact item. You want to get the dough tight enough to rise upwards rather than spreading outwards.

Shaping
Forming the dough into a taut, shaped loaf

The shaping is a continuation of the knocking back process, because you are still tightening the dough as you form it into a loaf, rolls or flatbreads. Whether you are creating an oval bloomer, a round cob or a long baguette, it is important to shape your loaf carefully, keeping it nice and taut and even as you roll, fold and/or flatten.

Proving
Raising the shaped loaf

This is an important stage and one that gives a much better loaf by developing its aeration and structure. Normally I use a sturdy plastic bag to cover the shaped dough when it is proving – simply put the whole tray inside. You want a roomy bag that won't touch the top of the dough once it has risen. In effect, you are putting the dough in a bubble so it can grow undisturbed, without forming a skin. You know when your loaf is ready for the oven by gently pressing it with a finger: the dough should spring back.

If you over-prove the loaf and it starts to crease and slump slightly, knock it back and shape the dough again, then let it prove once more.

Baking
Transforming the dough into a great-tasting bread with a good crust

A high temperature is important for bread-making. The temperatures I give in the recipes are for fan ovens. Ovens vary significantly, but if you are using a conventional oven, you should up the temperature by around 10–15°C.

The dough will continue to rise in the oven, then hold its shape and form a brown crust as the starch and natural sugars caramelise. If I want a shiny, crackling crust, for example with sourdoughs and bloomers, I put an empty roasting tin on the bottom shelf of the oven as it heats up, then pour in about 1 litre of water from a jug when I put the bread in. This creates a good steamy environment that helps the crust to form well.

What you're looking for is a good brown colour to give flavour and a crisp crust to your bread. Take the loaf out of the oven with a clean tea towel and tap the bottom. It should sound hollow. If it doesn't, the bread isn't quite ready, so put it back in the oven and check again after 5 minutes.

Cooling
Letting the steam in the loaf evaporate

Tempting as it is to eat your loaf hot from the oven, it is better to let it cool completely on a wire rack to let the steam out. It will finish cooking as it cools, and become more digestible and easier to slice or tear.

Once cooled, store your loaf in an airtight container such as a bag or bread bin to stop its moisture evaporating quickly and the loaf going stale. Never keep bread in the fridge: it dries it out too quickly. You can briefly revive staling bread by putting it in the oven so the outside crisps up, but you then need to eat the loaf straight away as it will be drier and staler afterwards.

CLASSIC BREADS

To start off, I'm going to take you through the fundamentals of baking and how to make bread. Once you've mastered the basic techniques used in these traditional loaves, you'll have the confidence to tackle anything. This is a chapter of classic British breads; all are delicious and form the basis of some of my favourite dishes.

The first loaf, a bloomer, gives you the basic proportions for a loaf of white bread: 500g flour, 10g salt, 7g yeast and 320ml water. The other loaves are variations on this basic formula, the proportions changing a little with the type of flour and other added ingredients.

As well as teaching you how to bake, this chapter takes you through the traditions of our bread through the centuries, from my modern spin on a Medieval flat trencher to a classic bloomer. My rye, ale and oat loaf explores the historic links between the baker, the brewer, the miller and the farmer that go back thousands of years. The farmer produced the grains for the miller's flour and the brewer's ale. The brewer produced the yeasty barm that made the bread rise and the ale. Then the baker brought everything together and produced bread for the community.

We've got a long and proud tradition of bread-making in this country and that is reflected in all the flours produced here, such as rye, wholemeal and spelt, as well as strong white bread flour. In times past, everyone from lords to peasants ate rye and wholemeal bread. Then white bread became the rich man's choice and the peasants had rough rye. But actually the poor man's diet could be good – full of vegetables and wholemeal and rye bread – and it was the aristocracy who went to spas in places like Bath because their diet was less than nutritious.

During the late 19th century and 20th century, white bread was everywhere. Now wholewheat, granary, rye and other wholegrain breads are back in favour because people realise they're more nutritious and are good for you as well as delicious to eat.

I like British loaves of all kinds – there is room for them all. Choose the ones you like to eat best and keep baking them to learn the secrets of dough. The more you practise, the better you'll get.

BLOOMER

If you're new to bread-making this is a good recipe to start with, as it shows you the key techniques you need to master. It's vital to knead the dough vigorously to develop the gluten and give the dough stretchiness, and to knock back and shape the loaf well. All this strengthens the structure so the dough can rise upwards without a tin. The loaf gets its name from the way it rises and 'blooms' like a flower in the oven. The term also describes the lustre you get with a well baked loaf that has a crisp crust.

MAKES 1 LOAF

500g strong white bread flour, plus extra for dusting

10g salt

7g fast-action dried yeast

40ml olive oil, plus extra for oiling

320ml cool water

Tip the flour into a large mixing bowl and add the salt to one side of the bowl and the yeast to the other. Pour in the oil and 240ml of the water and use the fingers of one hand to mix the ingredients together. Use a clawing action to stir the water into the dry ingredients, so you gather in all the flour. Once you've got going, add the remaining water a little at a time until you have a soft, sticky (but not soggy) dough and you've picked up all the flour from the sides of the bowl. You may not need to add all of the water; it will depend on the absorbency of the flour you're using. (Bear in mind that the dough will become less sticky as you knead.)

Pour a little oil onto a work surface. I use oil rather than flour to stop the dough sticking to the surface as it keeps the dough soft and does not alter the balance of flour to water. A wetter dough is harder to handle at first, but produces better bread. Knead the dough for 5–10 minutes (or longer if you're a beginner). It will become less sticky and eventually turn into a smooth ball with an elastic texture. The time this takes depends on how vigorous you are with the dough. It is ready when it is really stretchy: if you pull a piece of the dough between your fingers you should be able to stretch it to at least 20cm.

Put the dough in a lightly oiled large bowl. Cover with cling film or a tea towel and leave to rise until tripled in size – at least 1½ hours, but it can take up to 3 hours depending on the temperature. A slow rise develops a better flavour, so don't put it in a warm spot. The ambient temperature in most kitchens is between 18°C and 24°C, which is perfectly adequate.

Continued overleaf

Place the risen dough on a lightly floured surface. You now need to 'knock back' the dough by folding it in on itself several times and pushing out the air with your knuckles and the heels of your hands. Do this until all the air is knocked out and the dough is smooth.

To shape the dough into a bloomer, first flatten it into a rectangle, with a long side facing you. Fold the long side furthest from you into the middle of the rectangle. Then fold the long side closest to you into the middle, on top of the other fold. Turn the loaf over, so you have a smooth top with a seam along the base. Tuck the ends of the loaf under to make a rough oval shape. Rock the loaf gently so you form the loaf into its bloomer shape.

The bread is now ready to prove. This second rise of the shaped loaf is one of the secrets of great bread, enabling the dough to develop even more flavour as the yeast ferments and giving it a lighter texture. Put the loaf on a baking tray (lined with baking parchment or silicone paper if it isn't non-stick). Put the whole tray inside a large, clean plastic bag, making sure there is plenty of space above the surface of the dough so it won't touch the plastic when it rises. Leave the loaf to prove, or rise again, until doubled in size; this will take about 1 hour. To check when the bread is ready for the oven, gently press it with your finger: the dough should spring back. While the bread is proving, heat your oven to 220°C and put a roasting tray on the bottom shelf to heat up.

Lightly spray or sprinkle the bread with water. Dust with a handful of flour, smoothing it all over the top of your loaf with the palm of your hand. Be gentle – you don't want to knock any air out of the loaf.

Using a very sharp knife, make 4 diagonal slashes across the top of the loaf, 2–3cm deep and at a 45° angle. This gives your loaf the classic bloomer finish: on baking the loaf expands, so the slashes open up. If you do not slash the top, as the bread continues to expand once the crust has formed, cracks will form around the bottom of the crust.

Just before you put the loaf in the oven, pour about 1 litre water into the roasting tray. This will create steam when the loaf is baking and give it a crisp crust and a slight sheen. Place the loaf on the middle oven shelf and bake for 25 minutes. Lower the oven setting to 200°C and bake for a further 10–15 minutes, until the crust has a good colour. Hold the loaf in a tea towel and tap the bottom. If the loaf sounds hollow, then it is ready. Put the loaf on a wire rack and leave it to cool completely.

Kneading

Transferring the soft, sticky dough to an oiled work surface, ready for kneading.

Pushing the dough away, then folding and tucking the end into the middle.

Turning and continuing to knead the dough vigorously to develop elasticity.

The fully kneaded dough, forming a smooth ball with a taut skin.

Step photographs continued overleaf

Knocking back and shaping

Pushing the air out of the risen dough
with your knuckles to knock it back.

Turning the roughly shaped loaf over so
the seam is underneath.

Gently rocking the loaf back and forth
to create the classic bloomer shape.

The shaped bloomer ready to be lifted
onto a baking sheet for proving.

Preparing for baking

Spraying the surface of the loaf with
water before dusting with flour.

Gently smoothing the flour over the
surface of the dough with one hand.

Slashing the dough on the diagonal,
using a very sharp knife.

The classic bloomer, ready for the oven.

Grilled vegetable picnic loaf

Here is a sandwich with a difference: a whole bloomer scooped out and filled with grilled vegetables and mozzarella for slicing and sharing. Grilling the vegetables softens the flesh and intensifies their flavour. You can, of course, vary the vegetables as you like – just make sure you grill them until they have an intense roasted flavour. Perfect for a picnic or summer lunch, you make this tasty sandwich loaf the evening before.

SERVES 6–8

3 red peppers

3 yellow peppers

4 courgettes

2 aubergines

6 tbsp olive oil

1 day-old bloomer (see page 23) or other crusty white loaf

3 tsp sherry vinegar

1 garlic clove, crushed

2–3 balls of buffalo mozzarella, about 150g each

3–4 tbsp ready-made pesto

25g basil sprigs, leaves stripped and roughly torn

Salt and black pepper

Heat the grill to high. Quarter, core and deseed the peppers. Cut the courgettes and aubergines lengthways into 5–7mm thick slices. Place all the vegetables in a large bowl, toss with half the oil and season with salt and pepper. You will need to grill them in batches. Lay in a single layer on a large baking tray (peppers skin side up) and grill until softened and slightly charred, turning the courgettes and aubergines as they brown.

Cut the loaf horizontally in two, just below the score marks. Scoop out the soft bread from the centre, leaving a 2–3cm shell. Blitz half the bread to crumbs in a food processor or blender. (Use the rest for breadcrumbs or croûtons.)

Put the grilled peppers, courgettes and aubergines into separate bowls and divide the breadcrumbs between them. For the dressing, in a bowl, whisk the remaining oil with the vinegar, garlic and any juices from the baking tray. Divide the dressing between the vegetables, season again and toss each bowlful to mix everything together. Leave to stand for an hour to allow the vegetables and breadcrumbs to soak up the dressing.

Slice the mozzarella into rounds and pat dry with kitchen paper. Spread the pesto over the cut surfaces of the loaf. Layer up the filling ingredients on the base: start with mozzarella, add a layer of each grilled vegetable, scattering a little torn basil in between, and finish with mozzarella. Top with the bloomer lid, wrap tightly in cling film and refrigerate overnight.

Unwrap the picnic loaf and cut into thick slices to serve.

RYE, ALE AND OAT BREAD

I first made this on a trip to Redbournbury Watermill and Bakery, near St Albans, Hertfordshire. In this lovely restored mill, dating back to the 17th century, the flour is stoneground the traditional way, then turned into artisan loaves in the bakery. As much of the organic wheat is grown in nearby fields there are few 'food miles'.

Rye flour (mixed with strong white flour for a bit more lift) and a malty ale give this bread plenty of flavour and sweetness. The result is a tasty dense-textured loaf.

MAKES 1 LOAF

350g rye flour

150g strong white bread flour, plus extra for dusting

10g salt

10g fast-action dried yeast

50ml black treacle

140ml cool water

250ml full-flavoured pale ale, such as Shepherd Neame Spitfire

Olive oil for oiling

For the beer batter topping

150ml ale (use the same as the dough)

100g rye flour

Pinch of caster sugar

50–75g jumbo rolled oats (or pinhead oats)

Mix the rye and white flours together in a bowl and add the salt to one side of the bowl and the yeast to the other. Add the treacle, 100ml of the water and 200ml of the ale. Use the fingers of one hand and a clawing action to mix the ingredients together. Continue to add the remaining ale and water, a little at a time, until you have a soft, sticky dough and you've picked up all the flour from the sides of the bowl. You may not need all of the liquid but try to incorporate as much of it as you can, even though the dough will be sticky. Rye flour needs more liquid than white wheat flour.

Pour a little oil onto a work surface and place the dough on it. Knead the dough for 5–10 minutes (or longer if you're a beginner). It will become less sticky as you knead and eventually turn into a smooth ball with an elastic texture.

When the dough is smooth and stretchy, put it into a lightly oiled large bowl, cover with cling film or a tea towel and leave it to rise until doubled in size. This will take longer than white bread; possibly as long as 4 hours.

Meanwhile, make the beer batter topping. This helps form a crust and enhances the appearance and flavour of the loaf. In a bowl, mix the ale with the rye flour and pinch of sugar to form a smooth paste. Leave to one side.

Continued overleaf

Shaping the dough into a ball with
a smooth, taut surface.

Spooning the beer batter paste on top
of the loaf.

Smoothing the beer batter coating
evenly over the surface of the loaf.

Dusting the oat-coated loaf with flour
before proving.

Tip the risen dough out onto a lightly floured work surface and knock it back by folding it repeatedly in on itself to gently push out the air until it is smooth.

Flatten the dough out into a rough rectangle with your hands, then roll it out into a thick oblong. Fold the 2 shorter ends in towards the centre and press them down to get a chunky squarish shape. Turn the dough over so that the join is underneath.

Now you need to shape the dough into a ball on the work surface: place your hands on each side of the dough and slightly underneath it, then turn the dough around repeatedly to form it into a ball, tucking the dough underneath itself as you do so. This will create a loaf with a smooth, taut top and a rough underside.

Spoon the beer batter on top of the loaf and smooth it gently with your hands to form a thick, even layer. Sprinkle with the oats and dust with flour. Place the loaf on a baking tray (lined with baking parchment or silicone paper if it isn't non-stick).

Leave the bread to prove, or rise again, until doubled in size, about 1½ hours. The loaf is ready for the oven if the dough springs back when you push a finger into it. Meanwhile, heat your oven to 220°C.

Place the bread in the centre of the oven and bake for 25 minutes. Then lower the oven setting to 200°C and bake for a further 10 minutes until the loaf is golden brown and sounds hollow when tapped on the base. Transfer to a wire rack and leave to cool.

Kent plum and apple chutney

For me, a Ploughman's Lunch must have a good strong Cheddar and one other cheese, such as Stilton or Époisses. On the side I like some crisp apple, celery and radishes, with perhaps some caramelised onion and roasted peppers. A good pickle or chutney is, of course, essential. This is my favourite chutney, made every year by my wife Alex, using the plums and apples that grow in our garden in Kent.

MAKES ABOUT 2.5KG

900g tomatoes

700g plums

900ml malt vinegar

1kg dessert apples

250g onions, roughly chopped

4 garlic cloves, peeled

225g mixed dried fruit

1½ tbsp pickling spice

450g demerara sugar

4 tsp salt

To serve

Rye, ale and oat bread (see page 31) or other good bread

Cheddar and/or other cheese

Crisp apples

Watercress

Radishes and/or celery

Cut out the stalks from the tomatoes with a small, sharp knife. Put the tomatoes into a large bowl, cover with just-boiled water and leave for 1 minute. Drain and put into a bowl of cold water to cool, then take out and peel off the skin with your fingers or a small knife. Roughly chop the tomato flesh. Cut the plums into quarters and remove the stones.

Put the tomatoes, plums and vinegar into a preserving pan or other large, wide pan and place over a medium-low heat. Cook, stirring occasionally, for about 10 minutes until soft.

Meanwhile, quarter, peel and core the apples. Put into a food processor with the onions, garlic and dried fruit and blitz briefly to chop roughly. Tie the pickling spice in a piece of muslin to make a bag. Add the apple mixture to the pan, then add the spice bag, sugar and salt. Stir well. Simmer for 2 hours, or until the chutney is thick, stirring occasionally.

Meanwhile, sterilise some preserving jars: wash them thoroughly in very hot water, then leave to dry in an oven preheated to 100°C. (Or you can put them through your dishwasher on a hot cycle.)

Remove the spice bag from the pan. Pour the warm chutney into the sterilised jars. Seal with vinegar-proof lids. Store the chutney in a cool, dark place for at least 1 month to let the flavour mature before eating.

Serve the chutney with good bread, cheese(s), apple, watercress and radishes or celery.

STILTON AND BACON ROLLS

Bread and cheese are culinary bedfellows and these rolls bring in another good companion: bacon. There are two baking lessons to be learnt from this recipe. Firstly, because Stilton and bacon are salty, I'm adding less salt than usual. Secondly, I'm using butter instead of oil in the dough. When you knead a bread that contains butter or other fat-rich ingredients, such as cheese and eggs, use flour on the work surface, not oil.

MAKES 16 ROLLS

500g strong white bread flour, plus extra for dusting

7g salt

10g fast-action dried yeast

60g unsalted butter, at room temperature

320ml cool water

130g dry-cure back bacon rashers, rind removed

150g Stilton, at room temperature, crumbled

Put the flour in a large bowl and add the salt to one side of the bowl and the yeast to the other. Add the butter in small pieces and mix with your fingers. Add 240ml of the water and mix it into the other ingredients using the fingers of one hand and a clawing action. Now add the remaining water a little at a time until you have a soft, sticky dough and you've picked up all the flour from the sides of the bowl. You may not need to add all of the water; it will depend on the absorbency of the flour you're using.

Turn the dough onto a lightly floured surface and knead well for 5–10 minutes (or longer if you're a beginner). It will become less sticky as you knead and eventually turn into a smooth ball with an elastic texture.

When the dough is smooth and stretchy, put it into a large bowl. Cover with cling film or a tea towel and leave to rise until doubled or tripled in size – at least 1½ hours, but it can take up to 2 or even 3 hours.

In the meantime, heat your grill to medium-high and grill the bacon rashers for a minute or two on each side until cooked. Set aside to cool, then cut into small pieces (you need 90g).

Tip the risen dough out onto a lightly floured surface and knock back by folding it in on itself repeatedly until it is smooth and all the air has been pushed out. Use your hands to mix the crumbled Stilton and bacon into the dough, really crushing them in so they are evenly distributed.

Continued overleaf

Shaping the Stilton and bacon flavoured
dough into a long sausage.

Cutting the dough in half with a baker's
scraper to make it easier to divide up.

Cutting the dough into even-sized pieces
with the scraper.

Rolling the pieces of dough into balls
and positioning them on a baking tray.

Roll the dough into a long sausage and divide it into 16 equal pieces. The easiest way to achieve equal-sized rolls is to cut the roll in half first, then cut each piece in two, then repeat twice more. If you weigh the pieces you can be sure they are the same size and will cook evenly.

———

Now roll each piece of dough into a ball between the palms of your hands. Alternatively you can shape each one into a ball by rolling it around on the work surface using the cupped palm of one hand (or use both hands to shape 2 balls at a time).

———

Line 2 baking trays with baking parchment or silicone paper, unless you have good non-stick trays. Place a roll in the centre of each tray and arrange 7 rolls around it, so they are almost touching. The rolls will come together as they rise to form a tear-and-share loaf.

———

Put each tray of rolls inside a large plastic bag, making sure there is plenty of space above the rolls so they won't touch the plastic and stick to it as they rise.

———

Leave the rolls to prove, or rise again, until they have doubled in size and come together. This will take about 1–1½ hours. The dough is ready for the oven if it springs back when you push a finger into it. Meanwhile, heat your oven to 220°C.

———

Spray the rolls with water, using a spray bottle, and then dust with flour. Bake on the middle shelf of the oven for 15–20 minutes, or until the rolls are golden brown and sound hollow when tapped on the bottom. Transfer to a wire rack and leave to cool.

Celery soup

Bread and soup work so well together. I use my bread almost like a spoon to soak up the soup. Just as bread goes with cheese, cheese goes with celery and the soft sharpness of this soup is the perfect partner for my Stilton and bacon rolls.

Use fresh stock, or bouillon powder or a stock cube as you wish, but if you do use a ready-made product, season the soup judiciously, as these stocks can be overly salty.

SERVES 4

500g celery (about
6 stalks), with leaves
(400g trimmed weight)

1 large potato, peeled

1 large leek, trimmed
and washed

40g butter

600ml vegetable stock

200ml milk

150ml double cream

Salt and white pepper

To serve

Stilton and bacon rolls
(see page 37) or other
good bread

Trim the celery, reserving a few leaves for garnish. Roughly chop the celery and potato and slice the leek into rings.

Melt the butter in a medium saucepan over a medium-low heat. Add the prepared vegetables and stir to coat them in the butter. Cook gently for about 10 minutes to soften slightly but don't let them colour.

Pour in the stock and season with a little salt. Bring to the boil, then turn down to a simmer. Cover and cook gently for 20–25 minutes, until the vegetables are cooked.

Blitz the soup with the milk in a food processor until smooth; you may need to do this in 2 batches. Strain through a sieve into a clean pan. It really is worth doing this as it gives the soup a velvety texture.

Taste the soup at this stage and add more salt if needed and a pinch of white pepper. Reheat the soup to simmering point and stir in two-thirds of the cream.

Divide the soup between warmed bowls and garnish each portion with an extra swirl of cream and the reserved chopped celery leaves. Enjoy with Stilton and bacon rolls or other good bread.

RYE AND SPELT BREAD

Spelt is an ancient grain that has been around for thousands of years and recently come back into fashion. It has a nuttier taste than modern wheat flour but doesn't contain as much gluten so it is mixed with wheat flour to give the loaf some lift. The combination of spelt and rye gives the bread a lovely earthy taste.

This recipe uses the 'sponge' technique: some of the mixture is left to ferment overnight, then used as the base of the final dough. This long fermentation gives the loaf a distinctive flavour.

MAKES 1 LOAF

For the 'sponge'

50g strong white bread flour

100g rye flour

100g spelt flour

5g fast-action dried yeast

200ml cool water

For the dough

50g strong white bread flour, plus extra for dusting

100g rye flour

100g spelt flour

10g salt

5g fast-action dried yeast

20ml olive oil, plus extra for oiling

About 150ml cool water

For the 'sponge', combine the flours in a bowl, add the yeast and water and mix to a soft, sticky dough. Cover with cling film or a tea towel and leave to ferment overnight, or for at least 5 hours.

For the dough, add the flours to the fermented 'sponge' base, then add the salt to one side of the bowl and the yeast to the other. Add the oil and 100ml water and mix together with one hand. Add as much of the remaining water as you need to form a soft, sticky dough.

Spread some oil on a work surface and tip the dough onto it. Knead thoroughly for 10 minutes, or until you have a smooth, elastic dough.

Shape the dough into a ball and place in a lightly oiled bowl. Leave to rise until doubled in size, about 1½ hours. Meanwhile, oil a 1kg loaf tin.

Tip the risen dough out onto a lightly floured surface and flatten it down. Fold the dough in on itself several times, then fold the sides into the middle to form a rectangle and roll up to into a sausage, the length of the loaf tin. Place seam side down in the tin.

Put the tin in a roomy plastic bag and leave to prove for 1½–2 hours until risen above the rim of the tin. Meanwhile, heat your oven to 220°C.

Dust the top of the loaf with white flour and bake for 35–45 minutes, until golden brown and the loaf sounds hollow when tapped on the base. Tip the loaf out of the tin and leave to cool completely on a wire rack.

Pork, chicken and pistachio pâté

This nutty pâté goes really well with my rye and spelt bread as a satisfying autumn or winter dish. It is simple and rewarding to make but you can mess it up if you don't get the seasoning right. To check on this, fry off a spoonful, taste and then adjust the mixture accordingly. Use less salt if your bacon is very salty.

You need fairly fatty pork, so get a butcher to mince some pork belly or a piece of shoulder with some fat. Or you can mince the pork and chicken yourself, using a mincer or food processor.

SERVES 6

100g mushrooms

2 tbsp vegetable oil

½ onion, finely chopped

2 garlic cloves, finely chopped

50ml medium sherry

¼ tsp freshly grated nutmeg

1 tsp dried thyme

1–1½ tsp salt

½ tsp ground black pepper

225g minced chicken (1 large skinless breast)

325g minced fatty pork

50g shelled pistachio nuts

2 tbsp finely chopped flat-leaf parsley

1 medium egg, beaten

225g rindless streaky bacon rashers

To serve

Rye and spelt bread (see page 43) or other bread

Butter for spreading

Wipe the mushrooms clean and chop them fairly finely. Heat the oil in a frying pan and add the onion, mushrooms and garlic. Fry gently over a medium-low heat for about 10 minutes until soft. Add the sherry, nutmeg, thyme, salt and pepper. Let it bubble for a couple of minutes to drive off the excess liquid.

―――

Put the minced chicken and pork, pistachio nuts, parsley and beaten egg into a mixing bowl. Tip in the mushroom and onion mixture and use your hands to combine the ingredients thoroughly.

―――

Heat your oven to 180°C. Line a 1kg loaf tin from side to side with the bacon rashers, letting the ends overhang the sides of the tin. Spoon in the pâté mixture and pack firmly down. Fold the ends the rashers over the top of the pâté to enclose it completely.

―――

Bake on the middle shelf of the oven for 1¼ hours or until the bacon on the top is lightly browned, by which time the pâté will be cooked through. Set aside to cool, then refrigerate until ready to serve.

―――

Take the pâté out of the fridge 20 minutes before serving to bring it to room temperature.

―――

Dip a cook's knife in hot water, then run it around the sides of the pâté to ease it away from the tin. Turn the pâté out onto a board and cut it into thick slices. Serve with rye and spelt bread or other good bread, toasted if preferred, and butter.

TRENCHER BREAD

This is my modern version of a trencher, a Medieval bread that essentially acted as an edible plate. You can serve the trencher topped with various savoury mixtures but it is especially good with my garlic and pink peppercorn lamb (see overleaf). Colourful and substantial, it's a great dish to set in the middle of the table and the bread soaks up all the delicious meat juices.

The dough is made with a mix of flours and a small amount of yeast to ensure a slow, low rise that will give it plenty of flavour.

MAKES 1 FLAT LOAF

250g strong wholemeal bread flour

100g rye flour

150g strong white bread flour, plus extra for dusting

10g salt

½ level tsp fast-action dried yeast

340ml cool water

Olive oil for oiling

Mix the flours in a large bowl and add the salt to one side of the bowl and the yeast to the other. Pour in 250ml of the water and mix it in using the fingers of one hand. Now add the remaining water a little at a time until you have a soft, dense dough and you've picked up all the flour from the sides of the bowl. You may not need all of the water.

Pour a little oil onto a work surface and place the dough on it. Knead for 5–10 minutes until you have a smooth, elastic dough. As the dough is quite stiff, you will need to apply plenty of pressure. Put the dough in a lightly oiled bowl, cover with cling film or a tea towel and leave until at least doubled in size. This will take about 3 hours.

Tip the risen dough out onto a lightly floured work surface. Using your hands, push the air out of the dough and form it into a rectangle, like a pizza base and the size of your standard baking tray, about 33 x 23cm. Push your fingertips into the surface to make dimples, leaving a 1cm margin to act as a rim. Prick with a fork. This creates a plate with dips to catch juices from the food you are serving on top.

Line your baking tray with baking parchment or silicone paper and lift the dough onto it. Put inside a roomy plastic bag and leave the dough to prove for 1 hour. The dough is ready for the oven if it springs back when you push a finger into it. Meanwhile, heat your oven to 220°C.

Bake the trencher in the oven for about 30 minutes, until pale brown and cooked through. Let cool slightly, then top with whatever you fancy.

Trencher with garlic and pink peppercorn lamb

Lamb steaks are a great match for the hearty trencher. When you are chargrilling any meat, take it out of the fridge 20 minutes or so before cooking to bring it to room temperature. Always oil the meat rather than the griddle and make sure your griddle is really hot before you put the meat on. Don't move or prod the meat on the griddle – you want it to get a good chargrilled crust.

SERVES 4

1 rosemary sprig, leaves stripped and finely chopped

3 garlic cloves, crushed

Finely grated zest of 1 lemon

1 tbsp olive oil

4 boneless lamb leg steaks

175g green beans, trimmed

2 tbsp pink peppercorns, roughly crushed

50g watercress, trimmed

8 spring onions, trimmed and sliced

12 radishes, sliced

Salt and black pepper

For the dressing

3 tbsp crème fraîche

Juice of ½ lemon

1 tsp English mustard

To serve

1 freshly baked trencher bread (see page 47)

In a large bowl, mix together the rosemary, garlic, lemon zest and oil. Add the lamb steaks and turn to coat in the marinade. Cover and leave to marinate in the fridge for at least 30 minutes, or overnight if preparing ahead. Take the meat out of the fridge 20 minutes before cooking.

Add the beans to a pan of boiling salted water and cook for 2–3 minutes, until tender but firm to the bite. Drain and plunge into cold water to refresh, then drain well.

For the dressing, mix the ingredients together in a bowl and season with salt and pepper to taste.

Place a griddle pan on a high heat so it gets really hot. Remove the lamb from the marinade, sprinkle with the crushed pink peppercorns and season with a little salt.

Add the lamb to the hot griddle and sear for 2–3 minutes on each side, until cooked to your liking. Transfer the meat to a warm plate and set aside to rest for 5 minutes.

To serve, place the warm trencher on a large platter. Scatter the beans, watercress, spring onions and radishes over the top. Slice the lamb steaks and lay on top of the salad. Trickle over any meat juices and spoon over the mustard dressing. Add a grinding of pepper and serve.

MALT LOAF

A proper malt loaf has a light texture and is more like a risen bread than the dense, squidgy ready-made versions you find in supermarkets. This one has an excellent flavour. It's also exceptionally easy – just a brief knead to bring the ingredients together and one rise. Malt extract, which you can find in healthfood shops, provides some extra sugar for the yeast to feed on, but more importantly it gives the bread its distinctive taste.

MAKES 2 LOAVES

25g unsalted butter, plus extra for greasing

1 tbsp soft dark brown sugar

3 tbsp malt extract

2 tbsp black treacle

350g strong white bread flour, plus extra for dusting

100g strong wholemeal bread flour

8g salt

14g fast-action dried yeast

225g sultanas

250ml warm water

1 tbsp runny honey, warmed, to glaze

Grease two 500g loaf tins with butter. Place the butter, sugar, malt extract and treacle in a small saucepan and heat gently, stirring, until the butter has melted and the sugar has dissolved. Remove from the heat and set aside to cool.

Mix the flours together in a large bowl and add the salt to one side of the bowl and the yeast to the other. Scatter over the sultanas. Pour in the cooled malt syrup mixture and the warm water and mix well with a wooden spoon until thoroughly combined.

Turn the mixture out onto a floured surface and knead gently but thoroughly for a few minutes to bring the dough together.

Divide the dough in half. Roll each piece into a sausage, the length of the loaf tins, and place in the prepared tins. Put each tin in a roomy plastic bag that won't touch the top of the dough as it rises. Leave to prove for 2 hours until the dough has risen above the top of the tins. Meanwhile, heat your oven to 190°C.

Bake the loaves on the middle shelf of the oven for 25–35 minutes, until a skewer inserted into the centre comes out clean.

As you remove the malt loaves from the oven, brush the tops with the warmed honey to glaze. Leave in the tins for 5 minutes, then carefully tip out and place on a wire rack to cool. Slice the malt loaves and spread with butter to serve.

Step photographs overleaf

Adding the water and mixing the dough
using a wooden spoon.

Turning the soft, sticky dough onto
a floured surface, ready for kneading.

Kneading gently but thoroughly to form
a cohesive dough.

Dividing the dough in half.

Shaping the dough into sausages to fit in
the loaf tins.

Marmalade and malt loaf pudding

Bread and butter pudding has long been a sweet way of using up bread – it even appeared in Hannah Glasse's *The Art of Cookery Made Plain and Easy*, published in 1747. And marmalade dates right back to the 15th century – to an imported Portuguese fruit paste, which gradually evolved into today's popular preserve.

This is my take on the traditional pudding. You might like to serve it with a dollop of crème fraîche flavoured with orange zest to cut through the richness, but I prefer cream!

SERVES 8–10

2 malt loaves (see page 51), thinly sliced

50g unsalted butter, at room temperature, plus extra for greasing

6 tbsp coarse-cut marmalade

100g sultanas

900ml full-fat milk

300ml double cream

6 large eggs

75g caster sugar

3 tsp ground cinnamon

2 tbsp demerara sugar

To serve (optional)

300ml pouring cream

OR

200ml crème fraîche, mixed with the finely grated zest of 1 small orange

Butter a large ovenproof dish, about 30 x 23cm and 6cm deep. Spread the slices of malt loaf with butter, then with the marmalade, and cut into triangles. Arrange half of the bread triangles in the prepared dish. Scatter over half of the sultanas. Arrange the rest of the triangles neatly on top, overlapping them, and scatter over the rest of the sultanas.

Heat the milk and cream gently in a saucepan until almost simmering, then take off the heat and leave to cool slightly. Meanwhile, whisk the eggs, caster sugar and cinnamon together in a bowl. Gradually pour on the warm creamy milk, whisking as you do so. Continue whisking until the custard mixture is evenly combined.

Carefully pour the custard over the bread and sprinkle the demerara sugar on top. Leave the pudding to stand for 30 minutes before baking, to allow the bread to absorb the custard. Meanwhile, heat your oven to 180°C.

Bake the pudding in the oven for 30–40 minutes, or until the custard has set and the top is golden brown. Serve with pouring cream, or crème fraîche flavoured with orange zest if you prefer.

Note For a smaller family-sized pudding, to serve 4–5, use one malt loaf and half the butter, marmalade and sultanas. Use 325ml milk, 100ml cream, 2 large eggs, 25g caster sugar and 1½ tsp ground cinnamon. Assemble the pudding in a 1 litre baking dish, about 6cm deep. Bake as above, for 25–30 minutes.

SODA BREADS

The beauty of soda breads and bakes is their sheer ease. Soda bread is a great starting point for people new to baking who are initially afraid of kneading and shaping and the whole production of a risen yeast dough. It is also the ideal bread to bake if you are in a hurry.

When you make a soda bread you simply put the flour in a bowl, add the liquid and soda and then bring the ingredients together as you would a scone. You gather the mixture, fold it a few times and then shape the loaf: done. Literally two minutes. The hardest part is measuring out the ingredients!

In my childhood, my dad was the bread man, but mum made the soda bread because it was quick and simple. It was my nan who used to make crumpets raised with bicarbonate of soda. I must have been five or six years old when I first saw her make them – I was certainly below the level of the counter because I remember looking up at her, fascinated. I watched her scooping the batter from the bowl, then the smell rising from the baking rings and afterwards the fantastic taste. We ate our crumpets toasted and slathered with butter. Nothing else. Often the simplest things are the best.

Bicarbonate of soda began to be used as a raising agent from the early 19th century and baking powder after that. The modern form of baking powder was invented in 1843 by a Birmingham chemist, Alfred Bird, because his wife was allergic to yeast (and to eggs, hence his better-known invention, instant custard powder).

The Industrial Revolution meant more people had ovens at home and soda and baking powder were used in domestic baking. Instead of buying live yeast, convenient pots of these raising agents could be kept at home and used to make a variety of griddle bakes that could be eaten instead of yeast-risen breads, and cakes that were light and quick to prepare.

I'm giving you a wide range of risen breads and cakes here, from traditional soda bread and scones to crumpets and old-fashioned ginger parkin. All of them are family favourites that taste so much better when baked at home.

SODA BREAD

This is one of the quickest and easiest breads to make. As it does not contain yeast, there is no kneading or rising involved: you simply mix the ingredients together, shape the dough, let it rest while you heat up the oven, then bake.

Bicarbonate of soda (an alkali) and buttermilk (an acid), react together to create the carbon dioxide that makes the bread rise. Originally a by-product of butter-making, buttermilk has a slightly sour flavour that gives soda bread its distinctive taste.

MAKES 1 LOAF

250g plain wholemeal flour

250g plain white flour, plus extra for dusting

1 tsp bicarbonate of soda

1 tsp salt

420ml buttermilk

Put both flours into a large bowl. Add the bicarbonate of soda and salt and mix together. Add the buttermilk and mix with one hand or a wooden spoon to form a sticky dough.

Flour a work surface and tip the dough onto it. Gently roll and fold the dough for a minute or so to bring it together, but don't knead it. Shape the dough into a ball by turning it around repeatedly on the surface between your cupped hands. Flatten the ball gently with your hand.

Place the loaf on a baking tray (lined with baking parchment or silicone paper if it isn't non-stick) and dust with white flour. Using a large knife, score the loaf deeply, dividing it into quarters. Open them out slightly to allow the heat to get into the centre of the bread. They will join up again as the bread expands in the oven.

Set the loaf aside for 30 minutes, to allow the bicarbonate of soda to start to work. Meanwhile, heat your oven to 200°C. (If you are in a rush, you can bake the loaf as soon as the oven is hot.)

Bake the loaf on the middle shelf of the oven for 30 minutes, or until the crust is golden brown on top and pale brown at the base of the cross. The bread should sound hollow when tapped on the bottom.

Transfer the loaf to a wire rack and leave to cool completely. Soda bread is best eaten on the day it is made but it can keep for a day or two in a bag in the bread bin.

Step photographs overleaf

Rolling and folding the dough to bring
it together.

Rotating the dough between cupped
hands to shape it into a ball.

Flattening the ball of dough gently with
one hand.

Scoring the floured loaf deeply with
a cross, using a sharp knife.

The soda bread, dusted with flour and
rested, ready for the oven.

Irish rarebit

Soda bread was popular long ago in Ireland, especially in rural areas where a regular supply of barm (brewer's yeast) wasn't always accessible to the home baker.

Here I'm giving you an Irish spin on Welsh rarebit, using Irish cheese, spring onions and a splash of stout. Rarebit is one of those great comfort foods that can be thrown together at the last minute. The mixture also keeps well in the fridge, so you can have it on standby for a quick lunch or supper.

SERVES 6

150ml full-fat milk

1½ tbsp plain flour

400g strong Irish Cheddar, grated

160g medium-fine white breadcrumbs

1 tsp English mustard powder

120ml Guinness or other stout

2 medium egg yolks

4 spring onions, trimmed and finely chopped

6 slices of soda bread (see page 61)

Black pepper

Watercress, to serve

Preheat your grill to high. Warm the milk in a saucepan until almost simmering, then whisk in the flour. Bring to the boil, stirring constantly, then reduce the heat to a simmer and cook, stirring, for a minute or two. The mixture should be smooth and slightly thickened.

Add the grated cheese and stir over a low heat until it has melted. Add the breadcrumbs, mustard powder and stout. Continue stirring over the heat until the mixture comes together and leaves the sides of the pan.

Tip the mixture into a bowl and leave for a minute to cool slightly, then add the egg yolks and beat vigorously with a wooden spoon until well combined. Stir in the spring onions.

Toast the soda bread on one side. Spread the rarebit on the untoasted side and place under the hot grill until bubbling and golden brown. Add a grinding of pepper and serve, with watercress on the side.

STOUT BREAD

This tasty brown soda bread is baked in a tin to encourage the bread to rise up. Using some white flour with the wholemeal lightens the texture of the bread, while the stout gives colour and a full flavour. The buttermilk reacts with the soda to make the bread rise and adds a refreshing note. Starting the loaf off in a very hot oven helps the liquid in the dough turn to steam and pushes up the rise. An excellent loaf for sandwiches.

MAKES 1 LOAF

Sunflower oil for oiling

550g plain wholemeal flour, plus extra for dusting

200g plain white flour, plus extra for dusting

2 tsp bicarbonate of soda

2 tbsp dark brown sugar

1 tsp salt

300ml stout

220ml buttermilk

Oil a 1kg loaf tin.

Put both flours into a large bowl. Add the bicarbonate of soda, sugar and salt and mix together. Pour in the stout and buttermilk and mix well with one hand or a wooden spoon to form a sticky dough.

Tip the mixture onto a lightly floured surface and roll and fold the mixture gently but thoroughly (rather than knead it) to bring the dough together and form it into a cohesive sausage, roughly the length of the loaf tin.

Put the dough into the loaf tin. Set the loaf aside for 30 minutes, to allow the bicarbonate of soda to start to work. Meanwhile, heat your oven to 230°C. (If you are in a rush, you can bake the loaf as soon as the oven is hot.)

Bake the loaf in the centre of the oven for 10 minutes, then lower the oven setting to 180°C. Bake for another 25 minutes, or until the loaf is golden brown and sounds hollow when tapped on the base.

Leave the loaf to cool in the tin for 5 minutes, then turn out onto a wire rack and let it cool completely before slicing.

Smoked salmon pâté

Soda bread is delicious partnered with two of Ireland's most famous exports: stout and salmon. This quick and easy pâté is a good way to use the inexpensive packets of smoked salmon trimmings sold in supermarkets. Horseradish pairs brilliantly with smoked salmon and gives the pâté a bit of a kick. This easy recipe also works well with smoked mackerel in place of the smoked salmon.

SERVES 6–8

100g cream cheese

100ml crème fraîche

200g smoked salmon

Finely grated zest of 1 lemon

Juice of ½ lemon, or more to taste

1 tbsp creamed horseradish

2 tbsp dill leaves, finely chopped, plus extra leaves to garnish

Black pepper

To serve

Stout bread (see page 67) or other good bread

Lemon wedges

Caper berries

Put all the pâté ingredients, except the pepper, in a food processor and pulse briefly until evenly combined. Don't overwork the mixture; the pâté should still have some texture.

Taste the pâté to check the seasoning, adding a little pepper; you are unlikely to require salt as the smoked salmon usually provides enough. Add a little more lemon juice if you think it needs it.

Serve the smoked salmon pâté in individual bowls, garnished with dill and accompanied by slices of stout bread, toasted if preferred, lemon wedges and caper berries.

CRUMPETS

Crisp and golden brown on the outside, yet light and fluffy within, these are magical. Once you've tried making them, you'll never pick up a packet in the supermarket again. Crumpets do take a bit of practice to get right but you'll soon get the knack.

Strong flour gives the crumpets their stretch and rise, while plain flour lends softness. Both yeast and bicarbonate of soda are used for leavening. You will need at least four 7–8cm metal rings to contain the batter, which can be cooked in batches.

MAKES 10–12 CRUMPETS

175g strong white bread flour

175g plain white flour

14g fast-action dried yeast

1 tsp caster sugar

350ml warm milk

150–200ml tepid water

½ tsp bicarbonate of soda

1 tsp salt

Sunflower oil for cooking

Put both flours into a large bowl and mix in the yeast. In a jug, dissolve the sugar in the warm milk, then pour onto the flour mixture. Using a wooden spoon, beat the mixture until you have a smooth batter. This will take 3–4 minutes and is hard work because the mixture is stiff, but it is essential to develop the protein strength in the batter and will ensure the crumpets develop their characteristic holes as they cook.

Cover the bowl with cling film or a tea towel and leave to stand for about an hour. The mixture will rise and then begin to fall – you will see marks on the side of the bowl where the batter reached before it dropped. This indicates that the yeast has created its carbon dioxide and is now exhausted. The gluten will now have developed sufficiently to give the crumpets structure and enable them to rise and hold their shape.

In a jug, mix 150ml of the tepid water with the bicarbonate of soda and salt. Stir this liquid into the batter until evenly combined, then gradually stir in as much of the remaining water as you need to get a thick dropping consistency. Cover the bowl and leave the batter to rest for about 20 minutes. Little holes will appear on the surface and the batter will become a bit sticky.

Heat a flat griddle or heavy-based frying pan on a medium-low heat. Lightly but thoroughly grease the inside of at least four 7–8cm metal crumpet rings (ideally non-stick). Lightly grease the griddle or pan, using a crumpled piece of kitchen paper dipped in oil.

Continued overleaf

Ladling the batter into a greased
crumpet ring on the hot griddle.

The crumpet batter beginning to form
bubbles on the surface as it cooks.

The set crumpet with burst bubbles on
the surface, ready for turning.

Cooking the crumpet for a minute or
two on the second side.

It's a good idea to start with a trial crumpet. The first one is never the best, like the first pancake. Put a greased crumpet ring on the griddle. Ladle enough batter into the ring to come just below the rim; it should be about 3cm deep. The temperature of the pan is important: it is better to cook the crumpet lower and slower than hot and fast.

After 6–8 minutes, the bottom of the crumpet should be browned and the rest almost cooked through. You'll know when it is nearly ready once the top looks almost set and most of the bubbles that have formed on the surface have burst. You can slightly speed up the cooking by popping these bubbles as they appear, using the sharp tip of a knife. When the crumpet is ready, the bubbles will stay open rather than fill up with liquid batter.

Turn the crumpet over carefully, using two kitchen tools, such as a spatula and a palette knife. Leave the crumpet to cook for another minute or two, then lift it off the griddle onto a wire rack. Remove the ring (if it sticks, run a small, sharp knife around the outside of the crumpet to loosen it).

Now that you have fine-tuned the time and temperature needed for your batter, you are ready to cook the rest of the crumpets in batches.

Serve the crumpets straight away, split or whole, with plenty of butter. Alternatively, leave them to cool on the wire rack and toast them before enjoying with butter.

Eggs Benedict

Crumpets are delicious served simply with butter and jam as a teatime classic, but they also make an excellent base for a sweet or savoury topping. I love this dish for a special weekend brunch.

My recipe uses a cheat's method for making hollandaise. It's so easy that you can even do it first thing in the morning. Don't take your eggs straight from the fridge, though, or the sauce may split. You'll have more hollandaise than you need but it isn't practicable to make less; refrigerate the rest and use within a day or two.

SERVES 4

4 very fresh large eggs

2 tbsp white wine vinegar

8 rashers of maple-cured back bacon

For the hollandaise

250g unsalted butter

3 large egg yolks, at room temperature

1 tbsp water

Juice of ½ lemon

Salt and white pepper

To serve

4 crumpets (see page 71), freshly toasted and warm

Black pepper

First make the hollandaise. Melt the butter slowly in a small pan over a low heat. Place the egg yolks, water and lemon juice in a food processor. Blitz for 1 minute, then with the motor still running, very slowly trickle in the warm melted butter through the funnel. The sauce will slowly thicken. When all the butter has been incorporated, scrape down the sides of the bowl and give one final pulse (see note). Season to taste with salt and a pinch of white pepper. You will have a rich buttery sauce.

To poach the eggs, half-fill a large saucepan with water. Bring to the boil and add the vinegar, then lower the heat so the water is simmering. Break an egg into a ramekin or cup. Stir the water in the pan to form a whirlpool and slide the egg in. The white will wrap itself around the yolk. Quickly repeat with a second egg. Cook for 2–3 minutes, then remove with a slotted spoon and drain. Repeat with the other 2 eggs, swirling the water before you slide each one into the pan.

Meanwhile, preheat your grill to medium-high and grill the bacon rashers on both sides until cooked; keep warm.

Put each crumpet on a warm plate and spoon on some hollandaise. Lay a bacon rasher on top and add a poached egg. Spoon over the remaining sauce, add a grinding of pepper and the other bacon rasher, then serve.

Note If your hollandaise splits, spoon it into a jug and clean the food processor. Add another egg yolk, blitz briefly, then with the motor running, slowly add the split hollandaise and it should re-combine.

CHEDDAR AND ROSEMARY SCONES

If there's anything better than the smell of bread baking in your home, it's the smell of baking cheesy bread. These savoury scones can be spread with butter and eaten with soup or cheese, or you can use the mixture as a cobbler topping for a stew (see page 80).

I've used three types of flour: self-raising white and wholemeal flour to get the scones to rise, and a malted flour to give them a sweet dimension and extra flavour.

MAKES 6 SCONES

80g self-raising white flour

100g self-raising wholemeal flour

65g malted bread flour

Pinch of salt

1 tbsp finely chopped rosemary

150g Cheddar, grated

175ml full-fat milk

1 egg, beaten, for brushing

Plain flour for dusting

Heat your oven to 220°C. Mix the flours together in a bowl. Mix in the salt, rosemary and 100g of the grated cheese, using one hand. Add most of the milk, mixing with your hand or a wooden spoon until evenly combined. Slowly add enough of the remaining milk to form a soft paste; you may not need all of it.

Tip the mixture onto a lightly floured work surface and lightly fold it together to form a soft dough. Try not to over-work the mixture as this will make the scones tough.

Gently roll the dough with a rolling pin or flatten with your hands to a rough circle, about 2.5cm thick, to ensure the scones have a good height. Cut out 6 rounds, using an 8cm plain cutter. Use a swift downwards action to cut each scone and don't twist the cutter to release the scone from the rest of the dough, or you will inhibit the rise and the shape will be squiffy. You may need to re-roll the dough once or twice more to get all 6 scones, in which case gently press the trimmings together.

Brush the tops of the scones with beaten egg and sprinkle with the remaining cheese. Transfer them to a baking tray (lined with baking parchment or silicone if it isn't non-stick). Bake for 15–20 minutes until risen and golden brown.

Transfer the scones to a wire rack to cool. They are best eaten on the day they are made, ideally still warm from the oven. Alternatively these scones freeze well and you can warm them through to serve.

Step photographs overleaf

Mixing the dry ingredients together
with one hand.

Incorporating enough milk into the
mixture to form a soft paste.

Gently rolling the scone dough out.

Making sure the dough round is evenly
thick so the scones will be high enough.

Cutting out the scones, using
an 8cm cutter.

Brushing the top of the scones with
beaten egg.

Sprinkling grated cheese on top of
the scones.

The prepared scones, ready for the oven.

Beef cobbler

Scones aren't just for afternoon tea – they can make a fabulous topping for a hearty stew. This winter warmer has a wholemeal, cheesy cobbler crust made from my Cheddar and rosemary scone dough. Crisp and golden on the surface, yet deliciously soft and moist underneath as it soaks up the rich meaty juices, the scone cobbler is a great addition to the stew.

SERVES 6

900g stewing steak, such as chuck

3 tbsp plain white flour

6 tbsp vegetable oil

2 onions, sliced

2 carrots, cut into 2cm slices

2 celery stalks, cut into 2cm slices

1 leek, washed and cut into 2cm rings

1 tbsp tomato purée

600ml red wine

600ml beef stock

1 bay leaf

1 tbsp finely chopped parsley (optional)

Salt and black pepper

For the cobbler topping

1 batch of Cheddar and rosemary scone dough (see page 77)

Heat your oven to 180°C. Cut the beef into 3–4cm chunks. Put the flour in a large bowl and season with salt and pepper. Toss the beef in the seasoned flour so each piece is coated.

Heat half the oil in a flameproof casserole and brown the meat in batches over a high heat; do not crowd the pan. Set the browned meat aside.

Heat the remaining oil in the casserole and fry the onions, carrots, celery and leek over a medium-low heat, stirring occasionally, for about 10 minutes until softened and just coloured. Stir in the tomato purée and cook for another 2 minutes.

Pour the wine into the casserole and stir to deglaze, scraping up the tasty bits stuck to the bottom. Bring to the boil and simmer for a minute or so, then pour in the stock and add the bay leaf. Return the beef to the casserole, cover and cook in the middle of the oven for 1½ hours.

While the stew is cooking, gently roll out the scone dough and cut 6 scones for the cobbler topping (see page 77). Set them to one side after you have brushed them with egg and topped with grated cheese.

Take the casserole from the oven and place the scones on top of the stew. Turn the oven setting up to 220°C. Return the casserole to the oven and bake, uncovered, for 20–25 minutes, or until the scone cobbler topping is risen and golden brown. Sprinkle with chopped parsley, if you like, and serve.

SOFT TREACLE PARKIN

This recipe, written by Mrs Henry Norton, comes from an 1835 Yorkshire manuscript in the collection of one of Britain's top food historians, Ivan Day. The original recipe measures the ingredients in a breakfast cup (275ml capacity) and I have kept that measure in the ingredients list, but given metric equivalents.

Parkin can be eaten straight away but improves on keeping, so it is worth doubling up these quantities to make a big batch. With a strong taste of ginger, this recipe has a warm, satisfying flavour.

MAKES 9–12 PIECES

½ cup treacle (200g)

½ cup butter (140g), plus extra for greasing

½ cup (120g) soft dark brown sugar

2 cups (350g) medium oatmeal

20g ground ginger

1 tsp bicarbonate of soda

2 medium eggs, lightly beaten

1 tbsp cider vinegar or white wine vinegar (the original recipe uses gooseberry vinegar)

Grease a 20cm square baking tin, 4cm deep, with butter, or line with baking parchment.

Put the treacle, butter and sugar in a saucepan over a low heat until the butter has melted and the sugar dissolved, stirring occasionally.

Mix the dry ingredients together in a large bowl, then pour in the warm syrup mixture and stir until thoroughly combined. Finally stir in the eggs and vinegar.

Pour the mixture into the prepared baking tin, cover loosely and leave to stand for 30 minutes, to allow the bicarbonate of soda to start to work. Meanwhile, heat your oven to 150°C.

Bake in the middle of the oven for 1 hour, or until a skewer inserted into the centre comes out clean and the parkin has shrunk away slightly from the edges of the tin.

Leave the parkin to cool in the tin, then turn out. Wrap in greaseproof paper and store in a tin. Parkin improves on keeping but it can also be eaten straight away. Cut into squares or smaller pieces to serve.

Parkin crumble

I'm very partial to a good crumble. Your spoon taps the crumble and pushes through to the soft, juicy fruit and you get all that wonderful flavour and texture. Parkin makes an excellent and unusual crumble topping and adds a warming hint of ginger. It works equally well with plums, peaches and apricots.

I like to serve this pudding with a generous scoop of Cornish vanilla ice cream but you might prefer a dollop of cream.

SERVES 6–8

10 plums, or 8 peaches, or 12 apricots

2cm piece of fresh root ginger, peeled and finely grated

Finely grated zest of ½ lemon

Finely grated zest and juice of 1 large orange

1 vanilla pod

For the crumble topping

150g soft treacle parkin (see page 83)

30g demerara sugar

60g unsalted butter, cut into small pieces

Heat your oven to 180°C. Cut the fruit in half and prise out the stones. Arrange the fruit cut side up in an ovenproof dish, about 26 x 18cm. Scatter over the ginger and lemon and orange zest. Sprinkle with the orange juice.

Split the vanilla pod in half lengthways, scrape out the seeds and scatter them over the fruit in the dish. Tuck the pod halves in amongst the fruit.

Bake in the oven for 10–15 minutes, or until the fruit is starting to soften and release its juices.

Meanwhile, for the crumble topping, roughly crumble the parkin with your fingers into a bowl (or blitz briefly in a food processor to make large crumbs, then tip into a bowl). Add the sugar and butter and rub in lightly with your fingers.

When the fruit has softened, scatter the parkin crumble evenly on top. The buttery crumbs should almost but not completely cover the fruit in a thin layer (you are not looking for a thick blanket of crumble).

Return to the oven for another 10–15 minutes, or until the fruit is cooked and the fruit juice is bubbling up around the crumble topping.

FLATBREADS

These are the oldest of all breads, predating others because they can be cooked over a fire on a griddle or bakestone and don't need an oven. With such deep roots, it's no wonder that flatbreads are an important part of a country's culture and cuisine. I'm giving you recipes for flatbreads and dishes they partner from all over the world so you can enjoy their variety and versatility.

Flatbreads are a taste of history and even prehistory. The very foundation of risen breads came from flatbread. I wonder if someone left their flatbread dough unbaked one day so it bubbled up with wild yeasts from the air, then they stuck it on a griddle and saw how it rose beautifully. Over time, we went from flat to risen breads but never lost the taste for the old kinds and the knack of making them.

Roman soldiers used to travel with a bakestone and a grindstone so they could make their own flour and cook it into flatbread, wherever they were. An army marches on its stomach and this type of bread, quickly and conveniently made, provided good energy.

These simple breads are still common in nomadic or migrating cultures. When I was in the walled city of Petra in Jordan, I came across a Bedouin woman making flatbreads. She was squatting down on the ground next to a fire, making the breads on a small metal dome over the heat. I joined her and learnt how she did it. I was intrigued to realise that nothing had changed for thousands of years.

Because flatbreads date back to a time before cutlery, they can also be the plate and the cutlery, as well as the food. We still love wrapping food in flatbreads, be it steak, chicken or vegetables. Then there are the Mexican fajita-style wraps with guacamole, tomato salsa and soured cream added in too.

I'm going to show how easy it is to make some of our take-away favourites and tempt you to try different kinds of flatbreads. They are all relatively quick to make and delicious to eat.

PITTA BREADS

I think of pitta as a lunch carrier. In Cyprus, where I lived for six years, people use it to contain their souvlaki and other meats.

When you make pittas at home, the oven is like a magician's cave as you watch the dough puff up and transform into bread. The secret is to roll out the dough as thin as you can and to put the pittas onto a very hot baking tray. This ferocious initial burst of heat helps them puff up and cook properly.

MAKES 4–6 PITTAS

250g strong white bread flour, plus extra for dusting

5g salt

7g fast-action dried yeast

20g nigella or black onion seeds

160ml cool water

2 tsp olive oil, plus extra for oiling

Put the flour into a large bowl and add the salt to one side of the bowl and the yeast to the other. Add the nigella seeds, pour in 120ml of the water and add the 2 tsp oil. Mix the ingredients together, using the fingers of one hand. Add the remaining water a little at a time until you have a smooth, soft dough and you've picked up all the flour from the sides of the bowl; you may not need all the water.

Pour a little oil onto a work surface and place the dough on it. Knead for 5–10 minutes or until you have a smooth, elastic dough.

When the dough is soft, smooth and stretchy, shape it into a ball and place in a lightly oiled bowl. Cover and leave to rise until the dough has at least doubled in size – at least 1 hour. Meanwhile, heat your oven to 220°C (or higher) and put 2 baking trays inside to heat up.

Tip the dough onto a lightly floured surface and knock back by folding the dough in on itself repeatedly until all the air is knocked out. Divide the dough into 4–6 equal pieces and shape each piece into a ball. Flatten each ball with your fingertips, then roll into an oval, 5mm–1cm thick.

Take the hot trays from the oven, dust with flour and lay the pittas on them. Bake for 5–10 minutes until the breads puff up and just start to take on a hint of colour.

Wrap the pittas in a cloth, to trap the steam and keep them soft, and leave to cool. They are best eaten the same day, or they can be frozen.

Step photographs overleaf

The pitta dough risen to approximately twice its original size.

Turning the risen dough out onto a floured surface, ready to knock back.

Pressing the balls of dough with the fingers to flatten.

Rolling the flattened discs of dough into ovals, 5mm–1cm thick.

The pitta bread puffing up as it bakes
in the oven.

Souvlaki with Cypriot salad

Souvlaki is served as fast food in 'souvlatzidika', or souvlaki shops, in Cyprus and Greece. You buy one to take away and eat on the street, or sit in the shop and watch the world go by. Cubes of pork are cooked on a skewer with vegetables, then stuffed into pitta. It's a long established custom – there are even references to street vendors selling souvlaki in the ancient Greek city of Byzantium. You can either cook your souvlaki indoors on a griddle or outdoors on a barbecue.

SERVES 4–6

500g trimmed pork belly

2 red onions

1 red pepper

1 green pepper

1 tbsp olive oil

100ml red wine

2 tbsp dried oregano

Warm pitta breads
(see page 91)

Dollop of chilli sauce

Salt and black pepper

Lemon wedges, to serve

For the Cypriot salad

¼ white cabbage

1 Little Gem lettuce

1 red onion

3 ripe vine tomatoes

Handful of coriander leaves

1–2 handfuls of black olives

Juice of 1 lemon

2 tbsp extra virgin olive oil

200g feta cheese

If using wooden skewers, pre-soak them in water for 30 minutes (this stops them burning on the griddle).

For the salad, core and finely slice the white cabbage, shred the lettuce and finely slice the red onion. Toss together in a bowl. Cut the tomatoes into wedges and add to the bowl with the coriander leaves and olives.

To make the salad dressing, mix the lemon juice and olive oil together. Pour the dressing over the salad and toss through. Cut the feta into cubes and scatter over the salad. Season with salt and pepper to taste.

To make the souvlaki, cut the pork into 3cm cubes. Cut the red onions into wedges. Halve, core and deseed the peppers, then cut into roughly 3cm squares. Thread the pork onto skewers, alternating with the pepper pieces and onion wedges. Leave a slight gap between each item to help them to cook through.

Heat up a griddle over a high heat. Drizzle the skewers with oil and cook on the hot griddle, turning every few minutes to ensure even cooking.

Just before the meat is fully cooked, brush the skewers on the griddle with the wine, season with salt and pepper and sprinkle with oregano.

Once cooked, remove the griddled pork, peppers and onion from the skewers and serve in the warm pitta breads with a dash of chilli sauce, and the Cypriot salad and lemon wedges on the side.

CURRIED NAAN WITH SULTANAS

Traditional naan bread is baked on the side of a tandoor oven but you can make a very good version by cooking the flatbreads in a frying pan. My recipe includes curry powder, sultanas, mango chutney and fresh mango, so it's like a curry and a bread all wrapped up in one.

Everyone loves this bread, whether you eat it as a starter with a dip or serve it alongside a favourite curry, to mop up the juices.

MAKES 4 NAAN

250g strong white bread flour, plus extra for dusting

1 tbsp mild curry powder

5g salt

5g fast-action dried yeast

160ml tepid milk

Olive oil for oiling and frying

½ ripe but firm mango

50g sultanas

1 tbsp mango chutney

Put the flour and curry powder into a large bowl and add the salt to one side of the bowl and the yeast to the other. Pour in 140ml of the milk and mix together, using the fingers of one hand. Add as much of the remaining milk as you need to get a smooth, soft dough that comes away from the sides of the bowl.

Pour a little oil onto a work surface and tip the dough onto it. Knead for 5–10 minutes or until you have a smooth, elastic dough. Put into a lightly oiled bowl and leave to rise for 1 hour (it doesn't need to rise much).

Peel the mango and cut into 5mm cubes. Tip the dough onto a lightly floured surface and put the mango, sultanas and chutney on top. Knock back the dough to expel the air, incorporating the filling as you do so, by repeatedly folding the dough over the ingredients and pressing firmly.

Divide the dough into 4 equal pieces and shape each into a ball. Flatten each ball with your fingertips, then roll out into a circle, 3–5mm thick. Leave them to rest, covered with a clean tea towel, for 30 minutes.

Heat up a frying pan over a high heat, then add 1 tsp oil. Lay one circle of dough in the pan, pulling it through the oil as you do so to ensure it is lightly coated. Cook for a couple of minutes until the bottom is patched with brown, then turn over and cook the other side for a minute or two, pressing down a few times with a spatula. Once cooked, remove and keep warm in a cloth. Cook the rest of the naan in the same way, adding 1 tsp oil to the pan first each time. Eat warm with curry.

Step photographs overleaf

Incorporating the filling while
knocking back the dough.

Dividing the dough into 4 equal
pieces, ready to shape into balls.

Pressing the balls of dough to flatten
into discs with the fingers.

Rolling out the discs of dough into
rounds, 3–5mm thick.

The rested naan breads, ready to cook.

Chickpea curry

This delicious recipe was given to me by my friend, food writer and broadcaster Manju Malhi. She created it for me because she knows how much I love chickpeas. The array of spices give it a wonderful depth of flavour and I've included it here because it goes so well with my curried naan bread.

Don't be put off making it if you can't find mango powder or ground pomegranate seeds; just add 2 tsp tomato purée instead.

SERVES 4–6

2 x 400g tins chickpeas

2 large onions

6 tbsp vegetable oil

2 bay leaves

1 cinnamon stick

6cm piece of fresh root ginger, peeled

6 garlic cloves

1 tsp ground coriander

1 tsp ground cumin

½ tsp ground turmeric

¼ tsp chilli powder

½ tsp salt

¼ tsp mango powder (amchoor)

¼ tsp ground pomegranate seeds (anardana)

¼ tsp garam masala

500ml just-boiled water

To serve

Natural yoghurt

Coriander sprigs

Curried naan (see page 97)

Drain the chickpeas, rinse and set aside in the sieve. Finely chop the onions and set aside.

Heat the oil in a heavy-based saucepan over a medium heat, add the bay leaves and cinnamon stick and fry for 30 seconds, stirring constantly; don't let them burn.

Add the onions to the pan and fry for about 8 minutes until softened and golden, stirring from time to time to ensure they don't burn.

Finely grate the ginger and garlic, or whiz them together in a small food processor to a paste. Add to the pan with the ground coriander, cumin, turmeric, chilli powder and salt. Stir in the mango powder and ground pomegranate seeds (if you have them, or add 2 tsp tomato purée) and the garam masala. Cook for a further 2–3 minutes, stirring occasionally.

Now add the chickpeas and continue to stir for 5 minutes, mashing some of them against side of the pan with a wooden spoon to create a bit of texture in the sauce. Stir in the just-boiled water.

Leave the curry to simmer, uncovered, for 7–8 minutes, stirring from time to time, until the liquid has reduced down and thickened. Taste and add more salt if necessary.

Serve the curry topped with a swirl of yoghurt and a scattering of coriander. Accompany with warm naan, and your favourite chutney.

MANEESH

Maneesh is a classic flatbread from the Middle East, eaten as part of a mezze; it's also a popular breakfast bread. The dough is spread with za'atar, a strong mix of aromatic herbs and sesame seeds, then baked in a hot oven. As you bite into it the crunchy top is a lovely contrast to the softness of the dough inside.

I love the fact that this bread is a part of cultures that go back thousands of years and yet remains an everyday food of today.

MAKES 3 LARGE BREADS

500g strong white bread flour, plus extra for dusting

10g salt

25g caster sugar

10g fast-action dried yeast

20ml olive oil, plus extra for oiling

360ml tepid water

For the za'atar topping

3 tbsp sesame seeds

2 tbsp dried thyme

1 tbsp dried marjoram

2½ tbsp olive oil

Put the flour into a large bowl and add the salt and sugar to one side of the bowl and the yeast to the other. Add the olive oil and 270ml of the water. Mix the ingredients together, using the fingers of one hand. Add the remaining water a little at a time until you have a smooth, soft dough and you've picked up all the flour from the sides of the bowl; you may not need all the water.

Pour a little oil onto a work surface and place the dough on it. Knead for 5–10 minutes or until you have a smooth, elastic dough.

When the dough is soft, smooth and stretchy, shape it into a ball and place in a lightly oiled bowl. Cover and leave to rise until at least doubled in size – at least 1 hour.

Tip the dough onto a lightly floured surface and knock back by folding the dough in on itself repeatedly until all the air is knocked out. Divide into 3 equal pieces and shape each into a ball. Now roll each into a large circle, 23cm in diameter. Place on 2 or 3 baking trays (lined with baking parchment or silicone paper if they are not non-stick).

For the topping, in a bowl, mix the sesame seeds and herbs with the olive oil to a thick paste. Spread over the surface of the breads with one hand. Leave to rest for 20 minutes. Meanwhile, heat your oven to 230°C.

Bake the breads in the middle of the oven for about 15 minutes until golden. Transfer to a wire rack and leave to cool.

Baba ganoush

Known as 'poor man's caviar', this renowned aubergine dish is eaten throughout the Middle East. To get the full flavour of the dish it is important to chargrill the aubergine properly before it is mixed with the tahini, lemon juice and plenty of garlic.

Baba ganoush and maneesh is a classic pairing. The earthy taste of the aubergine marries with the aromatic flavours of the bread and you have a great contrast of textures. It's lovely as a starter or as part of a tableful of mezze.

SERVES 6–8

3 aubergines

3 garlic cloves

1 tsp salt

Juice of 1 lemon

2 tbsp tahini (sesame seed paste)

3 tbsp olive oil, plus extra to finish

1 tbsp roughly chopped flat-leaf parsley

Black pepper

To serve

Maneesh (see page 103) or pitta breads (see page 91)

Heat your grill to high. Prick the aubergines with a fork and grill them, turning occasionally, until the skin is charred and blackened all over and the flesh feels completely soft when you press them. Leave until cool enough to handle.

Meanwhile, crush the garlic together with the salt on a board, using the flat side of a knife, or use a pestle and mortar. The salt is abrasive and helps to form a smooth paste. Tip into a large bowl, add the lemon juice, tahini and olive oil and stir to combine. Season with black pepper.

Cut the aubergines in half. Scoop out the soft flesh and finely chop it. Add to the tahini mixture and stir well.

Spoon the baba ganoush into a serving dish and top with a drizzle of olive oil. Add a grinding of pepper and a scattering of chopped parsley and enjoy with maneesh or pitta breads.

WRAPS

I love wraps – they're such an easy way of eating and kids enjoy
them too. There are many different kinds, made with a variety
of flours, even ground up rice and lentils, but this is my simple
wrap, using wheat flour, that any beginner can master. I fry them
in a little olive oil until lightly coloured but still soft enough to
roll, but you can cook them in a dry pan if you prefer.

MAKES 6 WRAPS

250g strong white bread
flour, plus extra for
dusting

5g fast-action dried yeast

5g salt

15g caster sugar

20g unsalted butter,
softened

160ml cool water

Vegetable oil for oiling
and frying

Put the flour into a large bowl and add the yeast to one side of the bowl
and the salt and sugar to the other. Mix to distribute evenly through
the flour. Add the butter and use your hands to rub it into the flour.
Add 140ml of the water and mix together, using the fingers of one hand.
Add as much of the remaining water as you need to get a smooth, soft
dough that comes away from the sides of the bowl.

Pour a little oil onto a work surface and place the dough on it. Knead
well for 5–8 minutes or until you have a smooth, elastic dough.

Place the dough in a lightly oiled bowl, cover and leave to rise for
1½ hours (it doesn't need to rise much).

Tip the dough onto a lightly floured surface. Knock back the dough
to expel the air, by repeatedly folding it in on itself. Divide the dough
into 6 equal pieces. Shape each into a ball, then roll out very thinly
to a circle, 20cm in diameter.

Heat up a frying pan over a high heat, then add 1 tsp oil. Lay one circle
of dough in the pan and cook for 1½–2 minutes on each side until lightly
browned; don't let them get too dark or they will be firm and difficult
to roll. Once cooked, remove from the pan and keep warm in a cloth.

Cook the rest of the wraps in the same way, adding 1 tsp oil to the pan
first each time. Pile them on top of each other in the cloth to keep them
warm and soft. Eat warm with curry or other spicy dishes, or with dips.

Vegetable masala

I've based this vegetable masala on a curry I ate at an excellent South Indian restaurant in Leicester called Kayal. You can cook the vegetables fresh or use up leftovers, varying them according to what you have to hand. The mixture is thickened with mashed potato so it can be spread over a flatbread and rolled up; you could also thicken it with some cooked lentils.

SERVES 6

150ml vegetable oil

15 curry leaves, roughly torn if large

1 tbsp mustard seeds

3 onions, finely sliced

100g cabbage, finely sliced

400g mixed peas and diced carrots and green beans (or other vegetables)

2 tsp ground turmeric

2 tsp caster sugar

6 tomatoes

40g fresh root ginger, peeled and finely chopped

1 green chilli, deseeded if preferred for less heat, finely chopped

2 garlic cloves, finely chopped

About 250g cooked mashed potato

Salt

To serve

Wraps (see page 107)

Heat the oil in a pan and add the curry leaves and mustard seeds. Fry for a couple of minutes, stirring occasionally, until the mustard seeds start to pop.

Add the sliced onions, cabbage, mixed vegetables, turmeric and sugar. Stir everything together well, cover with a lid and cook over a medium-high heat for a few minutes, shaking the pan or stirring a couple of times to stop the vegetables sticking to the bottom of the pan.

Roughly chop the tomatoes and add them to the pan with the ginger, chilli and garlic. Lower the heat and cook for a further 5–10 minutes, or until the vegetables are cooked through. Stir in enough mashed potato to thicken the mixture and season with salt to taste. Cook until the potato is heated through.

Spread the masala on the wraps. Roll them up and enjoy, with your favourite chutney.

CORN TORTILLAS

The Mexican wraps or soft tortillas that you buy in a supermarket are made from wheat flour, but these are traditional corn tortillas made with Mexican maize flour, masa harina. This gluten-free flour, available online from specialist Mexican food suppliers, has a distinctive taste. You can substitute wheat flour, but masa harina will give you a more flavourful and robust tortilla.

In Mexico, this simple dough is often flattened in a tortilla press but these small tortillas are easily rolled by hand.

MAKES 18 TORTILLAS

190g masa harina

Pinch of salt

250ml warm water

1 tbsp olive oil

Vegetable oil for frying

Mix the masa harina and salt in a bowl. Add the water and olive oil, and mix with one hand until you get a smooth dough. This is tighter than a yeast dough and it feels quite crumbly; if it's too dry, add a few extra drops of water. This dough is for rolling, rather than stretching.

Divide the dough into 18 equal pieces and shape into small balls. Cover loosely with cling film and leave to rest in the fridge for 30 minutes.

To shape, place a ball of dough between 2 layers of cling film and roll to flatten, give it a quarter-turn, then roll and turn again, to keep a round shape. Continue rolling and turning until you have a small 3–5mm thin round. Repeat with the rest of the dough. This is the easiest way to shape the tortillas, but sometimes I simply bash them on the work surface with my hand to flatten them.

To cook the tortillas, lightly oil a heavy-based frying pan or flat griddle and place on a high heat. Cook the tortillas, a few at a time (depending on the size of your pan), for 1 minute or so on each side, keeping a close eye on them; you don't want them to get too brown. Use a palette knife to push down any small bubbles that appear on the surface.

Once cooked, remove the tortillas from the pan and wrap in a clean tea towel to keep them soft and warm. Stack them as they are cooked and eat as soon as possible.

Tortilla tower

For me, this dish is all about layers of texture and flavour. First you've got the tortilla – not the soft wheat one but the original crispy one they eat in Mexico. Then there is the creamy richness of the guacamole, the refreshing zing of the tomato salsa, the spicy chicken and the tang of the soured cream and cheese.

SERVES 6

18 freshly cooked corn tortillas (see page 111)

6 tbsp soured cream

200g Monterey Jack or strong Cheddar, grated

6 small coriander sprigs

3 spring onions, finely chopped

For the spicy chicken

8 chicken thighs, with bone

2 tsp celery salt

1 tbsp dried oregano

1 tsp dried chilli flakes

1 tsp garlic salt

2 tsp ground cumin

1 tsp smoked paprika

Finely grated zest and juice of 2 limes (spent lime halves saved)

Continued overleaf

First prepare the spicy chicken. Heat your oven to 180°C. Remove the skin from the chicken thighs (unless they are already skinned) and pat dry with kitchen paper.

Put the celery salt, oregano, chilli flakes, garlic salt, cumin and smoked paprika into a plastic food bag or large bowl with the lime zest and juice. Shake the bag so the lime and spices are well mixed together, or stir them together in the bowl until well combined.

Put the chicken thighs into the bag or bowl and turn to coat in the lime and spice mix. The lime is for flavour but it also helps the spice mix to stick to the chicken.

Place the coated chicken thighs in a roasting dish with the spent lime halves (to add extra flavour) and cook in the oven for 35 minutes, or until the juices run clear when you insert a knife into the thickest part of a thigh, indicating that it is cooked through.

While the chicken is in the oven, you can prepare the guacamole and tomato salsa (see overleaf).

Once the chicken is cooked, remove from the oven and set aside until cool enough to handle. Strip the chicken meat from the bone and shred it into small pieces. Place in a bowl.

Continued overleaf

For the guacamole

3 ripe avocados

3 tbsp soured cream

Finely grated zest and juice of ½ lime, to taste

Finely grated zest and juice of ½ lemon, to taste

1 tbsp olive oil

Salt and black pepper

For the tomato salsa

6 tomatoes

1 large red onion

2 red chillies

4 garlic cloves, peeled

Olive oil for drizzling

1 dried chipotle chilli

Small bunch of coriander, leaves stripped and finely chopped

Juice of 2 limes

To finish

Sliced spring onion

Coriander leaves

Pinch of sumac (optional)

To make the guacamole, cut the avocados in half, prise out the stones and remove the skin. Roughly chop the avocado flesh, place in a bowl and lightly crush with a fork. Stir in the soured cream, then the lime and lemon zest and juice, to taste, and the olive oil. Season with salt and pepper to taste.

To make the tomato salsa, heat your grill to high. Halve the tomatoes and cut the red onion into wedges. Place the tomatoes, cut side up, on a baking tray with the onion wedges, fresh chillies and garlic. Drizzle with oil. Place under the hot grill for about 10 minutes until charred.

Place all the grilled ingredients in a food processor and add the chipotle chilli, coriander and lime juice. Pulse briefly to a chunky texture. Season with salt and pepper to taste.

To assemble each tortilla tower, place a dollop of guacamole in the centre of each plate and place a tortilla on top (this stops the tortilla sliding about). Add a layer of guacamole, then shredded spicy chicken, then a spoonful of tomato salsa, followed by soured cream and a sprinkling of grated cheese. Repeat these layers 3 times so each tower has 3 tortillas interleaved with the various toppings.

Top each tortilla tower with spring onion slices and coriander leaves and finish with a sprinkling of sumac, if you like.

CONTINENTAL BREADS

There's a great passion for bread in Europe. First thing in the morning you don't think of going out to get a newspaper, instead you go out to get a baguette if you're in France, or a ciabatta in Italy, or a koulouri in Cyprus. You're not just buying a loaf, you're buying the basis of the day's food. Everything on the table in some way links back to the bread you eat with it.

I've learnt about making these breads by being alongside bakers from other countries, both abroad and working in Britain. We don't need translators. You can see what the others are doing: the language is dough. Different kinds of baking are like bus routes – there are many ways to get from A to B; what's important is the destination. I'm going to share the secrets that I've picked up along the way so you can get there too.

Given their status, it's interesting that some of the iconic continental breads have become universally popular comparatively recently. The 'baguette' gained prominence after a law was passed in France in 1920 that prevented bakers from going to work before 4am. A long, thin baguette could be prepared and baked relatively quickly, so fresh bread could still be ready for the breakfast table.

The 'ciabatta' is an even more modern success. It was patented in the 1980s by an ex-racing driver, Arnaldo Cavallari, to give the baguette a run for its money in the sandwich market. This explains its shape – it was designed to be filled. Pizza is another Italian classic that we have taken to our tables. Making your own pizza at home means you get a lovely crispy base and the topping can be anything you fancy. I've moved away from the classic tomato base to make original pizzas that are simple and delicious.

Some of these breads, notably the baguette and ciabatta, are a step up in skill level because they are relatively wet doughs that need careful handling. But don't be put off: I'll show you some straightforward tips and guide you step-by-step along the way.

MINI BAGUETTES

The classic French baguette is one of the most renowned breads and one of the longest. As it is too lengthy to fit in most domestic ovens, I've given a recipe for a mini version. You can buy a special baguette tray with a curved surface to get perfectly round loaves but it is fine to use a baking tray.

For a good baguette, a thorough knead to develop the elasticity of the dough is essential. You also need to shape the loaf well and bake it in a steamy oven to get a light crisp crust and soft interior.

MAKES 2 MINI BAGUETTES

250g strong white bread flour, plus extra for dusting

5g salt

5g fast-action dried yeast

2 tbsp olive oil, plus extra for oiling

180ml cool water

Semolina for dusting

Put the flour in a food mixer fitted with a dough hook. Add the salt to one side of the bowl and the yeast to the other. (You can make this dough by hand but as it is wet and difficult to handle – and needs a very long knead – I would highly recommend using a mixer.)

Start mixing on a slow speed and gradually add the oil and water. After 5 minutes, turn the speed up to medium and mix for a further 5–10 minutes, until you have a glossy, elastic dough that forms a ball on the dough hook and has a long, strong stretch when you pull it. You should be able to stretch a piece out by 30cm without it breaking.

Tip the dough into a lightly oiled bowl. Cover with cling film or a tea towel and leave to rise for 2 hours, or until at least doubled in size.

Mix equal quantities of white flour and semolina together for dusting and scatter on a work surface. Tip the dough onto the surface and knock back by pressing it down with the heels of your hands and then the tips of your fingers. Fold the dough in on itself several times to give it greater strength for rising.

Divide the dough into 2 equal pieces. You are now going to shape the dough to give it form and structure. Stretch each piece of dough into a long oblong, with a long side facing you. Fold the long edge furthest from you firmly down into the middle, then fold the bottom edge up into the middle and push it down firmly with your knuckles or fingertips.

Continued overleaf

Dividing the baguette dough into
2 equal pieces.

Folding the long edges of the dough
inwards and pressing the edges down.

Rolling the dough firmly to shape the
baguette, keeping it taut.

Applying a little extra pressure on the
ends of the roll to get the classic shape.

Turn each piece over and roll into a baguette shape, keeping the dough nice and taut as you do so and applying a little extra pressure on the ends to get the classic baguette shape. The top should be smooth with a seam running along the bottom.

Line a baking tray with baking parchment or silicone paper, unless you have a good non-stick tray. Dust the tray well with the flour and semolina mixture, then lift the shaped baguettes onto it.

Place the baking tray inside a roomy plastic bag that won't touch the dough as it rises. Leave to prove, or rise again, for about 1 hour until the baguettes have roughly doubled in size. Meanwhile, heat your oven to 200°C and put a roasting tray on the bottom shelf.

Just before baking, dust the baguettes with the flour and semolina mix. Now slash the tops 3 times with a sharp knife, using long diagonal strokes and cutting about 2cm deep. This helps the top of the dough to open out attractively and gives the baguette its characteristic appearance.

Pour 1 litre water into the roasting tray to create some steam, which helps to form the crust. Bake the loaves in the oven for 25 minutes, then lower the oven setting to 180°C and bake for a further 10 minutes, or until the baguettes are golden brown and have a slight sheen to them. Leave to cool completely on a wire rack.

Caramelised garlic baguettes with mozzarella

This is the ultimate garlic bread. With soft cloves of caramelised roast garlic baked into the bread, it tastes nothing like the packaged stuff. Roasting the garlic mellows and sweetens the flavour to delicious effect and you can give the dish an extra dimension by also roasting extra whole bulbs and halving them to serve alongside the cheesy garlic baguette slices.

MAKES 2 GARLIC BREADS

1 head of garlic

Splash of olive oil

Pinch of caster sugar

Strong white bread flour and semolina for dusting

1 quantity baguette dough, risen and ready to be shaped (see page 121)

1 ball of buffalo mozzarella, about 125g

For the tomato salad

30 cherry tomatoes

1 tbsp coriander leaves

Splash of olive oil

Salt and black pepper

Heat your oven to 200°C. Smash the head of garlic on a board to release the cloves. Separate them out and place in a roasting tin, still in their skins. Add a splash of olive oil and a pinch each of salt and sugar and toss together. Bake in the hot oven for 20 minutes, or until caramelised but not burnt. Leave until cool enough to handle, then squeeze the soft roasted garlic cloves out of their skins.

Mix equal quantities of strong white flour and semolina together for dusting and scatter on a work surface. After its first rise, tip the baguette dough onto the surface and add the roasted garlic cloves (or as many as you like, depending on how intense you want the garlic flavour to be). Knock back the dough by pressing it down with the heels of your hands and then the tips of your fingers. Fold the dough in on itself several times to give it greater strength for rising. As you knock back, squish the roast garlic into the dough.

Shape, prove, slash and bake the garlic dough as you would a normal baguette (see page 123). Allow to cool.

To make the tomato salad, halve the tomatoes and toss gently in a bowl with the coriander, olive oil and salt and pepper to taste.

When the bread is cooled, cut it into slices. Thinly slice the mozzarella, place on the bread slices and grill until melted and bubbling. Grind over some pepper and serve with the tomato salad.

Baguettes with flavoured butter and mozzarella

Here are some other ways to jazz up your mini baguettes with well-flavoured butters. If you don't use all the butter on the bread, wrap it up in cling film or foil and keep it in the fridge to use as a finishing flavour for fish or meat, or to melt on top of cooked vegetables or a jacket potato.

MAKES 2 MINI BAGUETTES

2 mini baguettes
(see page 121)

1 ball of buffalo mozzarella,
about 225g

Black pepper

**Watercress and
horseradish butter**

125g unsalted butter,
at room temperature

1–2 tsp freshly grated
horseradish, or 3–4 tsp
creamed horseradish

3 tbsp finely chopped
watercress leaves

Pinch of salt

OR

**Lime, chilli and coriander
butter**

125g unsalted butter,
at room temperature

1 tsp dried chilli flakes

Finely grated zest of 1 lime

2½ tbsp finely chopped
coriander leaves

Pinch of salt

To make either flavoured butter, mix all the ingredients together and leave for at least an hour to allow time for the flavours to infuse.

Heat your grill to high. Cut the mini baguettes into long, angled slices. Thinly slice the mozzarella. Toast the baguette slices on both sides.

Spread the baguette slices with the flavoured butter and cover with the mozzarella slices. Grind over some pepper and grill until the mozzarella is melting, then serve.

Variations

For baked flavoured bread, slice each bread almost to the bottom of the loaf (but not right through) and spread the flavoured butter inside the slices. Wrap the loaves in foil and bake at 200°C for 20 minutes or until the bottom is crisp and the butter has melted nicely into the bread.

For fried flavoured bread, cut the bread into slices. Melt the flavoured butter in a frying pan with a splash of olive oil and fry the bread until crispy and golden.

CIABATTA

A beautiful ciabatta is a joy to eat and to make, but it's a tricky dough to handle because you need to keep it very light and airy. Making a good ciabatta is all about developing the flavour of the fermented sponge base and building up the elasticity in the dough with a long knead – using an electric mixer makes this easier to achieve. An oiled container helps to shape the dough and keep its height during rising. And using a mixture of flour and semolina for dusting stops the dough sliding and spreading on the tray.

MAKES 2 LOAVES

400g strong white bread flour, plus extra for dusting

7g fast-action dried yeast

300ml cool water

2 tbsp olive oil, plus extra for oiling

7g salt

Semolina for dusting

Combine half the flour and half the yeast with half the water in a bowl. Beat thoroughly with a wooden spoon to make a thick batter. Cover and leave to rise and develop for at least 6 hours at room temperature. This fermented sponge gives a good flavour to the bread.

Tip the dough into a food mixer fitted with a dough hook. Add the rest of the flour and yeast, and the salt (don't put it on top of the yeast). Add the oil and remaining water and mix for 10–15 minutes, until the dough is stringy and soft. You should be able to stretch a piece out by 30cm.

Tip the dough into a well oiled, 3 litre, square plastic container (about 20cm square and 12cm deep). Cover with the oiled lid. Leave the dough to swell until it has risen to the top of the container, about 1–2 hours.

Dust a work surface heavily with a mixture of half semolina and half flour. Dust a non-stick or lined baking tray too. Very gently tip the square of dough out onto the dusted work top and cut into 2 equal pieces with a floured knife, keeping as much air in the dough as possible. Holding it by the ends, gently stretch each piece into a long ciabatta shape, carefully lifting it onto the baking tray as you do so. Dust the tops of the loaves.

Put the tray into a large, roomy plastic bag and allow the dough to prove again for another 15 minutes. Meanwhile, heat your oven to 220°C.

Bake the loaves in the oven for 30 minutes, or until risen and golden brown. Transfer to a wire rack to cool.

Step photographs overleaf

Gently turning out the risen dough onto
the flour and semolina dusted surface.

The ciabatta dough, ready for shaping.

Cutting the ciabatta dough in half
to make 2 loaves.

Stretching the dough to a long ciabatta
and lifting onto the dusted baking tray.

The flour and semolina dusted ciabatta,
ready for the oven.

Panzanella

This traditional Tuscan salad is a handy way to use up stale bread, or you can make it with a fresh ciabatta. The bread soaks up the lovely garlicky dressing and turns a simple, colourful salad into a much more substantial dish. The dressing seems to have a lot of garlic, but the bread takes it up and softens the flavour. Use less or more, to your taste.

SERVES 4–6

2 red peppers

2 yellow peppers

Olive oil for drizzling

800g ripe plum tomatoes

Small handful of green olives, pitted

1 tbsp capers, drained and rinsed

3–4 garlic cloves, crushed, to taste

3 tbsp red wine vinegar

225ml extra virgin olive oil

1 ciabatta (see page 129)

Large handful of basil leaves

Salt and black pepper

Heat your oven to 200°C. Place the peppers on a roasting tray, drizzle with olive oil and roast in the oven for 25–30 minutes, until softened but not too charred. Place the peppers in a large bowl, cover with cling film and set aside for about 20 minutes; the steam created will help to lift the skins.

Meanwhile, prepare the tomatoes. Cut out the tomato stalks. Pour just-boiled water into a large bowl. Plunge the tomatoes into the water for 45 seconds, or until the skins start to peel away. Lift them out with a slotted spoon and plunge into cold water, then drain. Peel away the skins with your fingers or a small knife. Cut the tomatoes into quarters, then scoop out the seeds into a sieve over a bowl. Put the tomato quarters into a serving bowl. Press the seeds in the sieve to release the juice.

Peel the roasted the peppers and take out the seeds. Cut the flesh into large strips and add to the bowl of tomatoes with the olives and capers.

For the dressing, add the garlic, vinegar and extra virgin olive oil to the reserved tomato juice and whisk to combine. Season with salt and pepper to taste. Rip the ciabatta into chunks and toss with the garlicky dressing to coat well. Leave for at least an hour to allow the bread to soak up the dressing.

Add the ciabatta to the tomatoes, peppers, olives and capers. Tear in the basil leaves and use your hands to gently combine all the ingredients. Grind over a little more pepper before serving.

PIZZA BASE

Pizza is so simple to make at home and everyone loves it. There are two secrets to great pizza: get your oven as hot as you can and get the base as thin as possible. If you have a bakestone you can put that (or your baking tray) in the oven to heat up – to give the dough an extra whack of bottom heat. In this case, you'll need to assemble your pizzas on a flat tray and confidently slide them onto the hot surface. And, if you can master the art of throwing the dough into the air, you'll get an extra thin base.

MAKES 3 BASES

250g strong white bread flour, plus extra for dusting

5g salt

5g fast-action dried yeast

2 tbsp olive oil, plus extra for oiling

180ml cool water

Semolina for dusting

Put the flour in a large bowl and add the salt to one side of the bowl and the yeast to the other. Add the olive oil and 150ml of the water and mix with the fingers of one hand. Add the remaining water a little at a time until you have a smooth, soft dough and you've picked up all the flour from the sides of the bowl; you may not need all the water.

Tip the dough onto an oiled work surface and knead for 5–10 minutes or longer, until you have a smooth, elastic ball of dough. Put into a lightly oiled bowl, cover and leave to rise for 1–2 hours, until at least doubled in size. Meanwhile, heat your oven to as high as it will go – at least 220°C.

Mix equal quantities of white flour and semolina together for dusting and scatter on a work surface. Transfer the dough to the surface and divide into 3 equal pieces. Shape into taut balls, dust the top of these with the flour/semolina mix, then flatten into rounds, pressing down with the heels of your hands and then your fingertips to expel the air.

The best way to get a thin pizza base is to roll out each ball into a circle, dusting as you go to stop the rolling pin from sticking, and then throw it up into the air with a flick of your wrist. This pushes the dough to the outside of the circle. Repeat several times and you'll have a thin disc with a slight rim. This takes practice! Otherwise, just use a rolling pin to roll each ball out into a circle, getting the dough as thin as possible.

Put the pizza bases onto baking trays and apply your chosen toppings, then bake straight away.

Step photographs overleaf

Gathering the risen pizza dough.

Transferring the dough to the flour and semolina dusted surface.

Shaping the dough into taut balls.

Dusting the balls of dough with the flour and semolina mix.

Pressing the dough to push out the
air and flattening it into a disc.

Rolling the dough into a thin circle,
dusting occasionally to prevent sticking.

Flicking the dough circle in the air and
spinning to thin it evenly.

Repeating the action until the dough
circle is evenly thin with a slight rim.

Parma ham, fig and Gorgonzola pizza

Instead of always putting a tomato base on your pizza, try more unusual combinations of other ingredients. Here, sweet caramelised onions and fresh figs work brilliantly with the saltiness of Parma ham and the powerful flavour and creamy texture of Gorgonzola. This pizza tastes as good as it looks.

MAKES 3 PIZZAS

1 tbsp olive oil, plus extra for drizzling

2 onions, thinly sliced

Strong white flour and semolina for dusting

1 quantity pizza base dough, risen and ready to shape (see page 135)

75–100g Gorgonzola

100g Parma ham, cut into large strips

3 ripe figs, cut into thin wedges

2 tbsp freshly grated Pecorino

A dash of good-quality balsamic vinegar

Black pepper

Handful of rocket leaves, to finish

Before you flatten your pizza bases, heat the olive oil in a frying pan over a low heat and add the onions. Cook gently until they are soft and sweet, stirring occasionally; this will take about 20 minutes.

Heat your oven to 220°C, or as hot as it will go. Dust a work surface with a mixture of equal parts strong white flour and semolina and roll out or throw your pizza bases to flatten (see page 135). Lift them onto 2 or 3 dusted baking trays.

Scatter the caramelised onions on top of the pizza bases. Crumble the Gorgonzola over them, then lay the Parma ham and figs pieces on top and scatter over the grated Pecorino.

Drizzle some olive oil over the pizzas and sprinkle on a little balsamic vinegar. Grind some black pepper over the top. Bake in the oven for 8–10 minutes until the topping is golden and the pizza bases are crisp.

Scatter rocket leaves on top of the pizzas and serve straight away.

Tartiflette pizza

Tartiflette is a hearty, well-loved potato bake from the French Alps that I've adapted into a pizza topping. I use Jersey or new potatoes because they are sweet and fresh tasting and cook quickly. I love Reblochon on this pizza but you could also use Brie or another flavoursome, oozy cheese. This is a substantial pizza with plenty of flavour that's perfect for a winter supper.

MAKES 3 PIZZAS

75g smoked lardons

1 large onion, thinly sliced

1 garlic clove, crushed

Strong white flour and semolina for dusting

6 Jersey or new potatoes, boiled and cooled

1 quantity pizza base dough, risen and ready to shape (see page 135)

1 tbsp chopped thyme

75–100g Reblochon (without rind) or other oozy cheese such as Brie

75ml double cream

Black pepper

Heat your oven to at least 220°C, or as hot as it will go.

Put the lardons in a frying pan and cook over a low heat so they start to release their fat. Add the onion and stir well. Cook over a low heat, stirring occasionally, for about 10 minutes until the onion is soft. Stir in the garlic.

Dust a work surface with a mixture of equal parts strong white flour and semolina and roll out or throw your pizza bases to flatten (see page 135). Lift them onto 2 or 3 dusted baking trays.

Thinly slice the potatoes and lay on the pizza bases. Scatter the lardons, onion and garlic on top. Sprinkle with the chopped thyme. Cut the cheese into thin slices and lay on top of the lardons. Drizzle the cream over the pizzas and grind over some black pepper.

Bake in the oven for 8–10 minutes until the topping is golden and the pizza bases are crisp.

Variation

To turn a pizza into a calzone, arrange the filling on the pizza base, fold the dough in half to enclose the filling and pinch round the edges to seal. Bake in the oven at 220°C for 20–30 minutes, or until brown and crisp.

PAIN DE SAVOIE

Here's a loaf that gives a taste of Alpine life. My family loves skiing and this appealing bread is based on ingredients from the Savoie region in France where we go. Delicious toasted or fresh, it can be eaten on its own, as a sandwich or with a fondue (see page 146). Or grill some more cheese on top – Reblochon or Comté – to take it to the next level. That's it: lunch sorted!

MAKES 1 LOAF

400g strong white bread flour, plus extra for dusting

100g rye flour

10g salt

8g fast-action dried yeast

20ml olive oil, plus extra for oiling

330ml cool water

150g lardons, fried and cooled

200g Comté cheese, cut into 1cm cubes

Mix the flours in a large bowl and add the salt to one side of the bowl and the yeast to the other. Add the olive oil and 250ml of the water and mix with the fingers of one hand. Add as much of the rest of the water as you need to form a soft dough; rye flour takes a lot of water so you should need most or all of it.

Tip the dough onto an oiled work surface and knead well for 5–10 minutes or more, until the dough is smooth and elastic. Add the cooled lardons, working them well into the dough. Form the dough into a ball and put in a lightly oiled bowl. Cover with cling film or a tea towel and leave to rise until at least doubled or trebled in size – at least 2 hours.

Turn the dough onto a lightly floured surface and divide into 3 equal pieces. Knock back by pushing down on the dough with the heels of your hands, then your knuckles and fingertips, and folding the dough in on itself several times. Form each piece into a ball.

Oil a 20cm springform cake tin. Roll out a ball of dough to a 1.5–2cm thick circle, to fit the tin and lay it in the bottom. Scatter over half of the cheese. Roll out a similar disc of dough and lay on top. Add the rest of the cheese. Roll out the final ball of dough and place on top. Dust with flour. Put the tin inside a roomy plastic bag and leave to prove for about 1 hour, or until well puffed up. Meanwhile, heat your oven to 220°C.

Bake the loaf in the oven for 30 minutes. Leave to cool in the tin for 10 minutes, then remove and transfer to a wire rack to cool completely.

Step photographs overleaf

Rolling out the first ball of dough to a round to fit in the prepared tin.

Laying the first round of dough in the bottom of the tin.

Scattering a layer of cheese over the middle round of dough.

Positioning the final layer of dough in the tin.

The puffed-up proved loaf, ready
for the oven.

Fondue

Fondue was very popular in Britain in the sixties and seventies, then the interest died down. In France it has never gone away, and with good reason.

Toast the bread for dipping if you like, to make it a good, crisp carrier for the fondue. Charcuterie is a delicious accompaniment too – I like to grill pieces of Parma ham and use the crispy shards to dip into the melted cheese. Serve with a good wine from Savoie.

SERVES 4–6

2 garlic cloves, cut in half

300ml white wine, preferably from Savoie

225g Beaufort, grated

225g Gruyère, grated

1 tsp cornflour, mixed with a little water

1 tbsp Kirsch

To serve

1 pain de Savoie (see page 143) or other rustic loaf

Parma ham and/or other cured meats

Cornichons

Rub the bottom of a fondue pan or other heavy-bottomed pan with the cut garlic cloves, then add the wine and heat until bubbling. Discard the garlic or leave it in, as you like.

Turn down the heat a little and add the grated cheeses, stirring all the time until the cheese melts into the wine.

Add the cornflour paste and cook, stirring, for a minute or so. It is essential to keep stirring the fondue to ensure the cheese doesn't stick to the bottom of the pan and burn. Stir in the Kirsch.

Meanwhile, cut or tear the bread into chunks (toast it first if preferred).

Put the fondue in the middle of the table and let everyone dip their bread into it. Accompany with the chunks of alpine bread, cold meats and cornichons.

A TRIO OF BISCOTTI

These crunchy, sweet Italian treats date back to the 13th century. The dough is baked in a log, then cut into slices and baked again so they dry and crisp up, hence the name biscotti, which means 'twice-cooked'. There are many different ways to flavour your biscotti. Delicious with tea or coffee, you can also enjoy them the traditional Italian way, dipped into Vin Santo or a sweet wine. These are three of my favourite biscotti flavourings.

MAKES 15–20 BISCOTTI

For the biscotti base

250g plain white flour (use an extra 30g for the chocolate biscotti), plus extra for dusting

½ tsp baking powder

250g caster sugar

2–3 medium eggs, beaten

Pistachio and cranberry flavouring

220g shelled pistachio nuts

125g dried cranberries

Finely grated zest of 1 lemon

OR

Hazelnut and date flavouring

200g skinned hazelnuts

125g stoned dates

Finely grated zest of 1 lemon

Continued overleaf

Heat your oven to 140°C (or 160°C for a non-fan oven, which is a better option for this recipe if available). Line a baking tray with baking parchment or silicone paper – I suggest you do this even if your tray is non-stick.

———

Mix the flour, baking powder and sugar together in a bowl. Stir in the beaten eggs, a little at a time, making sure each addition is incorporated before adding the next. Continue until you have a firm dough; it may not be necessary to add all of the egg. The dough shouldn't be at all sticky. If you are making the chocolate biscotti, add the extra flour and be careful with the amount of egg you add (as the melted chocolate will also add to the stickiness of the mixture).

———

Now it's time to add your chosen flavouring (the quantity for each of these is sufficient to flavour the whole batch of dough).

———

For the pistachio and cranberry biscotti, roughly chop the pistachio nuts and dried cranberries and add them to the biscotti dough with the lemon zest. Mix the flavouring ingredients in with your hands until they are evenly incorporated.

———

For the hazelnut and date biscotti, roughly chop the nuts, keeping them chunky (some can remain whole). Roughly chop the dates and add to the biscotti dough with the nuts and lemon zest. Mix in with your hands until well combined.

———

Continued overleaf

Mixing the melted chocolate into the biscotti dough.

Kneading the dough gently before shaping.

Rolling one portion of the dough out to a long log.

Cutting the baked biscotti logs into slices, ready to return to the oven.

OR

Chocolate, almond and orange biscotti

50g good-quality dark chocolate

135g blanched almonds

50g chocolate chips

Finely grated zest of 1 orange

½ tsp vanilla extract

For the chocolate, almond and orange biscotti, melt the chocolate in a bowl over hot water, then cool until tepid. Roughly chop the almonds. Add the melted chocolate to the biscotti dough and stir until evenly incorporated. Bring the mixture together to form a firm dough. Add the almonds, chocolate chips, orange zest and vanilla extract. Mix these ingredients in with your hands until well combined.

Once you have added your flavourings, turn the biscotti dough out onto a floured surface and knead gently, then divide in half.

Roll each piece of dough into a long log, about 4cm in diameter. Place both logs on your lined baking tray, spacing them at least 5cm apart as the mixture will spread a bit. Bake in the oven for 30–35 minutes.

Leave the logs to cool on the tray for 10 minutes to allow the dough to firm up slightly, then transfer to a board. Cut the logs, on the diagonal, into 2–3cm thick slices.

Place the slices, cut side up, on the lined baking tray. Return to the oven for 20–30 minutes, or until the biscotti are dry through to the centre, turning them over halfway through. Transfer to a wire rack and leave to cool completely. These biscotti keep well in an airtight container.

Biscotti with hot mocha dipping sauce

You might expect to have your biscotti with an espresso, but dipping them into a rich mocha sauce is a wonderfully indulgent option. As well as honey, I've added marshmallows to the sauce to give it a sticky consistency that makes it cling better to the biscotti. Use a good-quality chocolate for the sauce – it will make all the difference – ideally one with at least 70% cocoa solids.

SERVES 6–8

1 quantity biscotti of your choice (see page 149)

For the dipping sauce

150g good-quality dark chocolate (your favourite)

150ml double cream

100ml espresso coffee

100g small marshmallows (or large ones chopped up)

3–6 tbsp honey, to taste

To make the dipping sauce, combine all the ingredients in a heavy-based saucepan, adding as much honey as you like. This will depend on the type of honey you are using (dark single varietal ones, such as heather, have more flavour than lighter floral ones or blended honeys) and how sweet you want the dip. One tip for measuring out honey is to heat the spoon first by dipping it in very hot water, so that the honey slides off more easily.

Warm the ingredients together gently over a low heat. You will need to stir constantly, until all the marshmallows and the chocolate have melted and the mixture combines to form a homogeneous, smooth, glossy dipping sauce.

Serve the mocha dipping sauce warm or hot in espresso cups or little bowls with a few biscotti on the side to dunk in.

SOURDOUGH

Sourdough is the oldest form of leavened bread in the world. It looks different, it smells different and it has a distinctive and delicious taste. This is the vintage single malt of bread. It has real character and is incredibly satisfying to make.

Many people ignore sourdough because they think it is going to be tricky. It's true that making a sourdough for the first time can be a bit hit-and-miss. And then when you do get a good loaf, you might ask: 'How the hell did that happen?'. But in fact a sourdough is not so difficult once you understand the basics. The techniques used are largely the same as for other yeasted breads. Yes, they do take more time, but they're definitely worth the wait.

With sourdough there are fewer hard-and-fast rules than with the usual yeasted breads and the variables are mostly in your environment. Sourdoughs use a home-made starter culture to achieve the rise and flavour. Not surprisingly, this home-produced yeast is more sensitive than commercial yeast. It's a live material and will respond more definitely to its circumstances. In summer, your starter culture will be more active than it is in winter. If you live in a stone house in the Scottish Highlands a sourdough bread could take more than a day to rise properly; if you live in a small flat with the central heating on all day then it might take just four hours.

One key is to remember that the culture works best at 22–24°C. During the winter, add water to the dough that is baby-bath warm; during the summer, add cool or cold water. A dough thermometer can be useful to check the temperature.

I'll give you the basics of how to make a starter culture and get it ready to bake. Then I'll show you how to use it as the basis of your loaves. Once you begin to make sourdough bread, it becomes addictive, not just for the taste but also for the fascinating complexities and sense of 'aliveness' in how it works.

SOURDOUGH STARTER

A sourdough starter is essentially about producing yeast to make your dough rise and give it a great flavour. For this one, I'm using green grapes to help it get going, but you could use another fruit such as an apple. For the first week, treat your starter like a pet, don't just leave it alone. It's beginning to grow and you need to understand its characteristics and how it reacts to temperature variations. Look at it a couple of times a day to see what's going on and when it needs to be fed, or 'refreshed' with flour and water.

**MAKES 1 QUANTITY
SOURDOUGH STARTER**

250g strong white bread flour

5–7 seedless organic green grapes

250ml tepid water

For each refreshing

100g strong white bread flour

100ml tepid water

Put the flour in a mixing bowl. Chop up the grapes, add them to the flour, then pour in the water and mix to combine.

Tip the mixture into a large jar or a plastic box with an airtight lid that is roomy enough for it to rise. Cover and leave to ferment at warm room temperature (20–24°C is best) for 3 days. You should see the mixture froth up. One tip is to draw a line level with the top of the mixture using a black maker pen so you can see how your starter rises and falls.

After 3 days, the mixture should be risen, bubbly and slightly darker. When you open the lid, it will smell distinctly sour. This shows your starter is undergoing a lactic fermentation and is active. If it isn't working then discard half the mixture, add 100g flour, 100ml water and some more chopped grapes and leave it for another day or two.

Once your starter is active, discard half the mixture and stir in another 100g strong white flour and 100ml water (or enough water to keep it the same consistency). This is called 'refreshing' your starter and is what you do to feed the yeast. It needs to be done at least every few days to keep your starter alive.

Leave the refreshed starter for at least 24 hours and it should bubble up and become thick and almost jelly-like in texture. It is now ready to use to make your sourdough.

Continued overleaf

Adding the chopped grapes to the flour.

Pouring the water into the flour and grape mixture.

Mixing the starter with a wooden spoon until evenly combined.

The active starter, risen and dropped back in the jar, ready to be fed.

Storing and using your sourdough starter

If you make sourdough regularly, store your starter at room temperature in a place where you'll look at it once a day. Remember it is alive and needs to be fed.

———

You need to refresh, or feed, your starter at least every couple of days (it may be more often if it is particularly active). You'll need to add more flour and water in any case after you take some of the starter away to make a loaf.

———

The best time to feed the starter is after it has bubbled up and is starting to drop again. This tells you that the yeast has fed on the available food and will need more.

———

The starter should be like a thick batter. When you feed it, stir in about 100g strong white flour and enough tepid water to keep it to roughly the same consistency.

———

Unless you are making sourdough regularly, the best place to keep your starter is in the fridge. This will slow down the activity of the yeast but not kill it. A brown film will form on top, but don't worry about this. Just take the starter out of the fridge, stir in the film, discard half the starter and feed or refresh it as above with flour and water. Leave at room temperature and it should get going again.

———

If the starter is outside the fridge and seems to be inactive and has a brown film on top, throw half of the starter away, give it a feed and perhaps some chopped grapes and it should get going again.

———

Over time, the chopped grapes will disintegrate into the mixture. You can also fish them out and discard them once the starter has got going.

CLASSIC SOURDOUGH

Once you've got a good, active starter you are equipped to make a sourdough. With its lengthy rise and slow prove this loaf takes longer than other breads but it's well worth the wait. It has a lovely crust, a great chewy texture and a delicious tangy flavour. Sourdough requires a good knead and careful handling to develop the dough so it can rise and keep its height. A dusting mix of flour and semolina stops the dough sticking to the proving bowl or banneton and helps to prevent it spreading on the baking tray.

MAKES 1 LOAF

375g strong white bread flour, plus extra for dusting

250g sourdough starter (see page 159)

7g salt

130–175ml tepid water

Olive oil for oiling

Semolina for dusting

Combine the flour, starter and salt in a large mixing bowl. The amount of water you will need to add will vary according to your flour and the thickness of your starter. Add 110ml water initially and mix it roughly into the dry ingredients with one hand. Then mix in as much of the remaining water as you can in small amounts to get a soft dough.

Pour a little oil onto a work surface, then tip the mixture onto it. Knead thoroughly for 10–15 minutes or longer, until the dough is soft, elastic and smooth. The dough is ready when it is stretchy and starting to form a soft, smooth skin.

Tip the dough into a lightly oiled bowl and cover with cling film or a tea towel, or put into an oiled roomy plastic box with a lid. Leave to rise for 5 hours, or until at least doubled in size. The ideal temperature is 22–24°C; don't let it go cooler than 15°C or higher than 25°C.

Mix equal quantities of white flour and semolina together for dusting and scatter on a work surface. Tip the risen dough out onto the dusted surface. Push the dough down with your knuckles and the heels of your hands, then with your fingers to knock out the air. Fold the dough in on itself several times to strengthen its structure.

Flatten the dough down into a rough rectangle. Fold the two shorter ends in towards the centre and press them down to get a chunky squarish shape. Turn the dough over so that the join is underneath.

Continued overleaf

Now shape the dough into a ball: cup it with your hands on either side and turn it round and round, tucking the dough in slightly underneath as you go and pulling it in to create a ball with a smooth, taut top.

Dust your ball of dough with the flour and semolina mix. Dust a small round 500g banneton or smallish round mixing bowl generously too. The banneton gives a good appearance to the end loaf but a bowl will work fine. Tip the dough, smooth side down, into the dusted banneton or bowl (it must be very well dusted or the dough will stick when you turn it out).

Put the banneton or bowl inside a large, roomy plastic bag, making sure there is plenty of space above the surface of the dough so it won't touch the plastic when it rises. Leave the dough to rise for 4–8 hours, or until at least doubled in size. The dough is ready when it springs back if you push a finger into it. Don't rush the proving; it's an important stage for the development of the flavour and structure of the end loaf.

Heat your oven to 220°C. Put a roasting tin on the bottom shelf as the oven heats up. Heavily dust a non-stick baking tray, or one lined with parchment or silicone paper, with the flour and semolina mix. Very gently tip the loaf onto the baking tray, trying to keep its domed shape. Slash the top with a sharp knife.

Pour 1 litre water into the roasting tin in the oven. This creates steam in the oven and helps the crust form well. Bake the loaf for 30 minutes, then lower the oven setting to 200°C and bake it for a further 15–20 minutes until the loaf is golden brown and sounds hollow when you tap it on the base. Transfer to a wire rack and leave to cool completely.

Kneading

Mixing the dough with the hands, using a clawing action.

Starting to knead the soft, sticky dough on a lightly oiled surface.

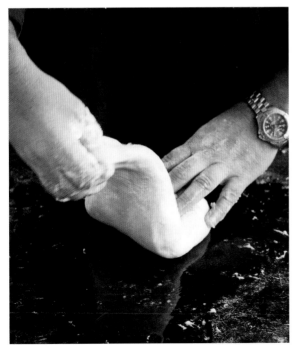

Stretching and folding the dough to knead it thoroughly.

Placing the ball of dough in a lightly oiled bowl ready to prove.

Step photographs continued overleaf

Knocking back and shaping

Pushing down on the dough with the
knuckles to knock out the air.

Pushing the dough down with the heel
of the hand to knock it back further.

Folding the dough in on itself repeatedly
to strengthen its structure.

Rotating the dough with the hands
to shape it into a smooth ball.

Preparing for baking

Putting the dough into a banneton,
well dusted with flour/semolina.

Placing the dough in a large, roomy
plastic bag to prove.

Gently tipping the proved loaf out onto
the prepared baking tray.

Slashing the top of the dough with
a sharp knife.

Breakfast ham and eggs with grilled tomato

Sourdough makes exceptional toast and there's no better way to use it than in a proper cooked breakfast. My ultimate breakfast is scrambled eggs with crispy Parma ham and chargrilled beefsteak tomatoes. This is a morning feast worth making time for – enough to satisfy one very hungry person, or two with moderate appetites.

SERVES 1–2

1 beefsteak tomato

Olive oil for drizzling

3 slices of Parma ham

1–2 slices of sourdough bread (see page 163)

3 medium eggs

50ml double cream or milk

Salt and black pepper

Butter, for spreading

Heat up a ridged griddle pan or heavy-based frying pan until hot. Cut the tomato in half, or into 3 pieces if it is very large. Season with salt and pepper, drizzle with olive oil and place on the hot griddle pan with the Parma ham. Cook for a few minutes on each side, turning once, until the tomato is charred and softened and the Parma ham is crispy, then remove to a warm plate.

While the tomato and ham are on the griddle, lightly toast the sourdough slices and start making the scrambled eggs.

For the scrambled eggs, crack the eggs into a bowl, season with salt and pepper, add the cream or milk and beat well to combine. Pour into a small non-stick pan and cook over a very low heat until scrambled, stirring constantly and carefully once the curd has started to form, making sure you reach the edges of the pan. The eggs are ready when they have a sloppy consistency. Take the pan off the heat just before they are done (they will cook a bit more after you take them off).

Spread the sourdough toast with butter, then lay on warm plate(s). Spoon the scrambled eggs onto the toast and add the Parma ham. Place the grilled tomatoes on the side, add a grinding of pepper and serve.

BASIL AND CORIANDER SOURDOUGH

Any well-made sourdough will have a fantastic taste, and fresh herbs give yet another dimension. For an attractive appearance I deeply score the loaf into eighths – the slashes open out like petals on top of the loaf as the dough expands.

This is a lovely rustic bread to tear into pieces or cut into wedges – great for dipping into home-made soup. Alternatively, you can slice the loaf and toast it to bring out yet more of its herby sourdough flavour.

MAKES 1 LOAF

375g strong white bread flour, plus extra for dusting

250g sourdough starter (see page 159)

7g salt

130–175ml tepid water

Handful of chopped basil

Handful of chopped coriander

Olive oil for oiling

Semolina for dusting

Combine the flour, starter and salt in a large mixing bowl. The amount of water you will need to add will vary according to your flour and the thickness of your starter. Add 110ml water initially and mix it into the dry ingredients with one hand. Then mix in as much of the remaining water as you can in small amounts to get a soft dough. Mix in the herbs.

Pour a little oil onto a work surface, then tip the mixture onto it. Knead thoroughly for 10–15 minutes or longer, until the dough is soft, elastic and smooth. The dough is ready when it is stretchy and starting to form a soft, smooth skin.

Tip the dough into a lightly oiled bowl and cover with cling film or a tea towel, or put into an oiled roomy plastic box with a lid. Leave to rise for 5 hours, or until at least doubled in size. The ideal temperature is 22–24°C; don't let it go cooler than 15°C or higher than 25°C.

Mix equal quantities of white flour and semolina together for dusting and scatter on a work surface. Tip the risen dough out onto the surface. Push the dough down with your knuckles and the heels of your hands, then with your fingers to knock out the air. Fold the dough in on itself several times to strengthen its structure.

Flatten the dough down into a rough rectangle. Fold the two shorter ends in towards the centre and press them down to get a chunky squarish shape. Turn the dough over so that the join is underneath.

Continued overleaf

Tipping the risen sourdough out onto
the dusted surface, ready for shaping.

Starting to shape the sourdough into
a ball.

Scoring the loaf deeply, using
a baker's scraper.

The proved loaf, its slashes opened up
decoratively, ready for the oven.

Now shape the dough into a ball: cup it with your hands on either side and turn it round and round, tucking the dough in slightly underneath as you go and pulling it in to create a ball with a smooth, taut top.

Heavily dust a baking tray with plenty of the flour and semolina mix. Put the shaped loaf on the dusted tray. Dust the top of the loaf with the flour and semolina mix. Use a baker's scraper or a large sharp knife to deeply slash the top of the loaf, first in a cross and then into eighths. This is for decoration rather than dividing up the end loaf into segments; the dough will come together as the loaf proves.

Put the tray inside a large, roomy plastic bag, making sure there is plenty of space above the surface of the dough so it won't touch the plastic when it rises. Leave the dough to rise for at least 4 hours, or until at least doubled in size. The dough is ready when it springs back if you push a finger into it. Don't rush the proving; it's an important stage for the development of the flavour and structure of the end loaf.

Heat your oven to 220°C. Put a roasting tin on the bottom shelf as the oven heats up.

Pour 1 litre water into the roasting tin in the oven. This creates steam in the oven and helps the crust form well. Bake the loaf for 30 minutes, then lower the oven setting to 200°C and bake it for a further 15–20 minutes until the loaf is golden brown and sounds hollow when you tap it on the base. Transfer to a wire rack and leave to cool completely.

Roasted tomato and fennel soup

My wife Alex often prepares this chunky tomato soup. Not only is it warming and delicious, it's also incredibly straightforward. Everything is cooked together on a roasting tray, then whizzed up – there's no need for stock. A thick soup like this calls for a robust bread and my herby sourdough is the ideal partner. The basil and coriander play with the fennel and tomato so all four of them work together in synch.

SERVES 4–6

2kg ripe tomatoes

1 fennel bulb

1 small carrot, roughly chopped

6 garlic cloves

60ml olive oil, plus extra to serve (optional)

1 tbsp balsamic vinegar

Handful of basil leaves

Sea salt and black pepper

To serve

Basil and coriander sourdough (see page 171)

Heat your oven to 200°C. Cut the tomatoes in half and place cut side up on a roasting tray. Cut the fennel into quarters and add to the tray with the carrot and garlic cloves. Drizzle with the 60ml olive oil and the balsamic vinegar and season generously with salt and a good grinding of pepper. Mix well.

Cover the roasting tray loosely with foil and bake for 1½ hours, or until the ingredients are well cooked. Remove the foil, then roast, uncovered, for a further 15–20 minutes to caramelise the juices slightly.

Blitz the contents of the roasting tray in a blender with half the basil leaves to a smooth, silky texture (you may need to do this in 2 batches). Taste and adjust the seasoning if you need to.

Serve the soup immediately in warm bowls, drizzled with a little more olive oil, if you like. Scatter the rest of the basil over the soup and add a grinding of pepper. Serve with wedges of basil and coriander sourdough.

OLIVE SOURDOUGH FOUGASSE

A French fougasse looks great and is easy to tear apart and share out. It's also easier to make than a classic sourdough loaf because you don't need to worry about shaping the dough into a dome. You just need to take care that the bread doesn't dry out because it is thin. The addition of juicy olives makes it deliciously savoury and moist. It is lovely alongside soups or salads, but my favourite way to enjoy an olive fougasse is torn and dipped into tapenade (see page 179), the famous Provençal olive paste.

MAKES 2 LOAVES

375g strong white bread flour, plus extra for dusting

250g sourdough starter (see page 159)

7g salt

130–175ml tepid water

Olive oil for oiling

Semolina for dusting

1 tbsp dried oregano

100g pitted black olives

100g pitted green olives

Combine the flour, starter and salt in a large mixing bowl. The amount of water you will need to add will vary according to your flour and the thickness of your starter. Add 110ml water initially and mix it roughly into the dry ingredients, using one hand. Then continue to add and mix in as much of the remaining water as you can in small amounts to get a soft dough.

Pour a little oil onto a work surface, then tip the mixture onto it. Knead thoroughly for 10–15 minutes or longer, until the dough is soft, elastic and smooth. The dough is ready when it is stretchy and starting to form a soft, smooth skin.

Tip the dough into a lightly oiled bowl and cover with cling film or a tea towel, or put into an oiled roomy plastic box with a lid. Leave to rise for 5 hours, or until at least doubled in size. The ideal temperature is 22–24°C; don't let it go cooler than 15°C or higher than 25°C.

Mix equal quantities of white flour and semolina together and use to heavily dust a work surface. Tip the risen dough out onto the dusted surface and scatter over the oregano and olives. Knead them into the dough thoroughly, really pushing the olives in so they break up a little. This will take a few minutes to do properly. At the same time, you are knocking back the dough, eliminating the air and folding it in on itself to improve the structure.

Continued overleaf

Dividing the olive sourdough into
2 even pieces.

Pressing the dough out into
a rough rectangle.

Cutting short diagonal slashes down
each side with a pizza cutter.

Stretching the dough a little to open out
the slashes.

Divide the dough into 2 pieces and shape each one into a fougasse. To do this, press and stretch out each piece into a rough rectangle. Make 4 diagonal cuts on both sides of each fougasse (a pizza cutter is a good tool for this, or use a knife). Pull the gaps open (they will close up a bit as the bread proves).

Line 2 baking trays with baking parchment or silicone paper, unless you have good non-stick trays. Carefully lift a fougasse onto each tray and dust with the flour and semolina mix.

Put each tray inside a large, roomy plastic bag, making sure there is plenty of space above the surface of the dough so it won't touch the plastic when it rises. Leave the dough to rise for at least 4 hours, or until at least doubled in size. The dough is ready when it springs back if you push a finger into it.

Heat your oven to 220°C. Put a roasting tin on the bottom shelf as the oven heats up.

Pour 1 litre water into the roasting tin in the oven. This creates steam in the oven and helps the crust form well. Bake the loaves for 20 minutes, or until golden and crispy. Transfer to a wire rack to cool.

Tapenade

To make this Provençal olive paste, put 25g drained anchovies in oil, 200g pitted black olives, 35g capers, 1–2 peeled garlic cloves, ½ tsp Dijon mustard, 1 tsp lemon juice and a small handful of basil leaves, chopped, into a food processor. Add 1–2 tbsp good olive oil and a grinding of pepper and blitz until chopped and well combined but not puréed. Taste and add more lemon juice and pepper if necessary. Transfer the tapenade to a clean jar, cover with a lid and store in the fridge. It will keep for a couple of weeks.

Tuna niçoise

I love a salade niçoise. The classic combination of tuna, potatoes, green beans, tomatoes, anchovy and olives makes me think of summer in the Mediterranean. Here my olive sourdough fougasse smeared with home-made tapenade provides the anchovy and olive elements. There are several parts to this dish but they can be prepared in advance and assembled quickly just before you want to eat.

SERVES 4

4 tuna steaks, each 125–140g

4 medium eggs

200g green beans, trimmed

200g new potatoes, cooked and cooled

4 Baby Gem lettuces

24 baby plum tomatoes

4 tsp capers, drained and rinsed

1 tbsp chopped chives

1 tbsp olive oil

Salt and black pepper

For the dressing

2 tsp Dijon mustard

½ tbsp white wine vinegar, or more to taste

100ml extra virgin olive oil

Juice of ½ lemon

To serve

1 olive sourdough fougasse (see page 177)

Tapenade (see page 179)

Have the tuna ready at room temperature. Add the eggs to a pan of simmering water and cook for 5 minutes (or 7 minutes for firm yolks), then drain and plunge into cold water. Peel, halve and set aside. Blanch the green beans in boiling salted water for a couple of minutes; drain, refresh in cold water, then drain and set aside with the potatoes.

To make the dressing, shake the ingredients together in a clean jam jar, with a little salt and pepper, to emulsify. Taste and adjust the seasoning and/or acidity with a little more vinegar if needed.

For the salad, roughly tear the lettuce leaves and place in a bowl. Halve the tomatoes and add to the bowl with the potatoes, beans, capers and chives. Drizzle 2 tbsp dressing over the salad and toss gently. Place in a large serving bowl or individual bowls. Place the eggs around the salad.

To cook the tuna, heat a griddle pan until hot. Rub a little olive oil on both sides of the tuna steaks and season with salt and pepper. Sear the tuna for 2 minutes on each side or until cooked to your liking.

Cut the olive sourdough fougasse into pieces and put the tapenade into a small serving bowl (you probably won't use the full amount).

To serve, slice the seared tuna on the diagonal and lay on top of the salad. Spread tapenade on some of the fougasse pieces and arrange around the edge of the salad. Serve the remaining fougasse, tapenade and dressing on the side, so people can help themselves.

WHITE CHOCOLATE AND RASPBERRY BREAD

Sourdough makes wonderful sweet breads. This white chocolate and raspberry bread is a great alternative to a teabread and can also be used as the basis for an indulgent pudding.

The fresh raspberries will add some extra liquid to the dough. Remember this when you are adding the water and hold back a little, so you end up with a manageable, soft dough – unless you are very confident in kneading wet doughs. Don't use frozen raspberries; they give out too much water.

MAKES 1 LOAF

375g strong white bread flour, plus extra for dusting

250g sourdough starter (see page 159)

7g salt

130–160ml tepid water

Olive oil for oiling

150g white chocolate chips

100g fresh raspberries

Semolina for dusting

Combine the flour, starter and salt in a large mixing bowl. The amount of water you will need to add will vary according to your flour and the thickness of your starter. Add 110ml water initially and mix it roughly into the dry ingredients with one hand. Then mix in as much of the remaining water as you can in small amounts to get a soft dough. Bear in mind that the raspberries you will add later release juices into the dough and this will make it wetter.

———

Pour a little oil onto a work surface, then tip the mixture onto it. Knead thoroughly for 10–15 minutes or longer, until the dough is soft, elastic and smooth. The dough is ready when it is stretchy and starting to form a soft, smooth skin.

———

Tip the dough into a lightly oiled bowl and cover with cling film or a tea towel, or put into an oiled roomy plastic box with a lid. Leave to rise for 5 hours, or until at least doubled in size. The ideal temperature is 22–24°C; don't let it go cooler than 15°C or higher than 25°C.

———

Mix equal quantities of white flour and semolina together for dusting. Scatter a generous layer of the flour and semolina mix on a work surface. Tip the risen dough out onto the dusted surface. Push the dough down with the heels of your hands and knuckles, then with your fingers to knock out all the air. Add the white chocolate chips and raspberries, kneading them well into the dough. Fold the dough in on itself several times to strengthen its structure.

———

Continued overleaf

Kneading the raspberries and white chocolate into the risen dough.

Folding the dough in on itself to strengthen as you knock it back.

Lifting the dough into the liberally dusted banneton.

The shaped loaf, placed seam side up in the banneton, ready for proving.

Heavily dust a 1kg loaf tin or a 500g long banneton with the flour and semolina mix. Roll the dough into an elongated shape, the length of the tin or banneton. Carefully lift the dough into the tin or banneton, placing it seam side up.

Put the banneton or bowl inside a large, roomy plastic bag, making sure there is plenty of space above the surface of the dough so it won't touch the plastic when it rises. Leave the dough to rise for at least 4 hours, or until at least doubled in size. The dough is ready when it springs back if you push a finger into it. Don't rush the proving; it's an important stage for the development of the flavour and structure of the end loaf.

Heat your oven to 190°C. Put a roasting tin on the bottom shelf as the oven heats up.

Line a baking tray with baking parchment or silicone paper, unless you have a good non-stick tray. Liberally dust it with the flour and semolina mix; this will help stop the dough spreading out. Quickly invert the banneton or loaf tin onto the tray. If it has been well dusted, the dough should fall out. If not, you'll have to give it a bit of help, but try to keep as much air in the loaf as possible.

Pour 1 litre water into the roasting tin in the oven. This creates steam in the oven and helps the crust form well. Bake the loaf for 45 minutes until it is golden brown and sounds hollow when you tap it on the base. Transfer to a wire rack and leave to cool completely.

Summer pudding with white chocolate cream

My white chocolate and raspberry sourdough gives a whole new dimension to a classic summer pudding. The recipe works best with bread that is a day or two old because the dry crumb soaks up the fruity juices better. If you use fresh bread, reserve some of the juice to brush over the outside of the pudding to even up the colour if necessary. Make sure you line your pudding basin well, patching up any gaps.

SERVES 6

450g raspberries

350g other mixed soft fruit (blackberries, redcurrants, blackcurrants etc.)

150g caster sugar

100ml raspberry liqueur or Kirsch

Vegetable oil or butter for greasing

8–10 crustless slices of white chocolate and raspberry bread (see page 183), ideally 1–2 days old

For the white chocolate cream

100g white chocolate, in pieces

150ml double cream

250g mascarpone

2 tsp icing sugar, plus extra to decorate

Combine the fruit, sugar and liqueur in a saucepan and heat gently for 5–8 minutes, or until the juices have reduced a little. Take off the heat.

Grease a 1 litre pudding basin. Carefully line the base and sides of the basin with four-fifths of the bread slices. Overlap the bread slightly to avoid gaps between them and press the edges together. Use extra, small pieces to fill any gaps.

Spoon the fruit and juices into the bread-lined bowl, keeping back a couple of tablespoonfuls of the juices. Cover with a layer of bread, pressing the edges onto the rim of the bread lining the sides.

Cover the pudding with cling film and place a small plate on top that just fits inside the rim of the bowl. Press down firmly and put a small weight on top. Leave in the fridge overnight.

To make the white chocolate cream, melt the chocolate in a heatproof bowl over a pan of barely simmering water, making sure the bottom of the bowl does not touch the water. Once melted, take off the heat and allow to cool slightly, then gently stir in the cream. Stir in the mascarpone, then the icing sugar.

To serve, run a knife around the edge of the pudding to ease it away from the bowl, then turn out onto a deep plate. Brush any parts of the bread where the juices haven't soaked all the way through, using the reserved juices. Serve with the white chocolate cream.

ENRICHED BREADS

An enriched dough is one enhanced with ingredients such as milk, sugar and eggs, and sometimes butter or lard. These doughs require careful handling and cooking as they are easy to burn or overcook. That said, once you know what to watch for, these rich breads are straightforward to make and a treat to eat.

Enriched breads are also where baking gets dramatic – many are created to be the centrepiece of the table. A beautiful brioche couronne served alongside a good salad is a meal in itself, while a plateful of home-made Danish pastries will turn a brunch or morning coffee into a special occasion.

This final chapter shows how the dividing lines between what is bread, cake and pastry are somewhat blurred. Before baking powder and bicarbonate of soda were invented in the 19th century, all cakes were risen with yeast. Britain is very much a bread country and cakes were like sweet, enriched loaves. Lardy cake is a well-known yeasted cake that we still eat but there used to be many others.

The tradition of enriched dough baking has prevailed rather more elsewhere. Cultures all over the world still sweeten their bread to celebrate special occasions and festivals. There are many famous sweet breads, such as the eastern European kulich, the German kugelhopf and the Italian panettone. I've given you a recipe for a Sicilian lemon and orange sweet bread that's a version of an Easter celebration cake, and my satsuma and dark chocolate brioche is one that my family enjoys at Christmas.

One of the secrets of enriched breads is to allow them time to rise properly. You've got to get your core dough right and then allow it to rise and prove fully. The slowness of proving enriched doughs makes people frustrated, but you need to be patient and give them time.

The fat in these enriched breads means they keep for a bit longer than normal breads, though somehow they don't stay on the table for long. Once your friends and family smell them cooking, they tend to drift towards the kitchen and you'll have trouble keeping them away!

DANISH PASTRY DOUGH

I use this versatile classic dough to make all kinds of savoury and sweet pastries, even croissants. Essentially it is a yeasted dough that's layered with butter and gives excellent results. This is not the time to stint on ingredients. Use the best quality butter you can. Normandy butter is the one I use as it has a higher melting point than other butters, which keeps the butter firm for as long as possible in the oven as the pastry cooks. Wrapped in cling film and sealed in a bag, this dough can be frozen for up to 6 months.

MAKES ABOUT 1KG

250g unsalted Normandy butter

500g strong white bread flour, plus extra for dusting

7g salt

80g caster sugar

10g fast-action dried yeast

260ml full-fat milk

1 medium egg, lightly beaten

Roll out the butter between 2 pieces of greaseproof paper to a rectangle, about 30 x 15cm and 8mm thick. Chill in the fridge for about 2 hours.

Put the flour in a large bowl, add the salt and sugar to one side of the bowl and the yeast to the other. Pour in most of the milk and the egg and mix with one hand until you have a soft mixture. If there are dry flakes in the bowl, add a few more drops of milk to bring the dough together.

Tip the dough out onto a lightly floured work surface and knead well for 10 minutes or until it is smooth and soft and can be stretched with your hands. (It will be slightly firmer and less stretchy than a bread dough.) Wrap in cling film and leave to rest in the fridge for at least 2 hours.

On a lightly floured surface, flatten the dough down with your knuckles, then roll out to a rectangle, about 50 x 20cm. Lay the flattened butter over two-thirds of the dough. Bring the unbuttered section over into the centre, then fold the other third over the top. You will have 3 layers of dough and 2 layers of butter. Pinch the sides of the chunky rectangle together slightly to stop the butter escaping when you roll out the pastry next time. Wrap in cling film and rest in the fridge for 30 minutes.

Give the chilled dough a quarter-turn, then roll out to a rectangle, about 50 x 20cm, as before. Fold into three, wrap and chill again. Repeat this turning, rolling, folding and chilling process twice more.

Wrap the dough in cling film and leave it to rest in the fridge overnight.

Step photographs overleaf

Kneading

Kneading the pastry dough by folding it in on itself repeatedly.

Continuing to knead the dough well to develop elasticity.

Pressing the rested dough down, using the knuckles, to flatten it.

Rolling out the flattened dough, applying firm, even pressure.

Rolling and folding

Folding the rectangle of dough into three to enclose the sheet of butter.

Rolling out the rested dough to a rectangle, keeping the edges straight.

Folding the rectangle of dough neatly into three again, to build up the layers.

Rolling the fully layered dough out for a final time before shaping as required.

Emmenthal, onion and mushroom pastries

Served still warm from the oven, these special savoury pastries make a delicious brunch or lunch. The crucial point is to keep the pastry cool, so make sure the mushroom and onion filling is cold before you assemble them. If the pastry is warmed, the butter will melt and leak out of the pastry in the oven and the pastries won't have that lovely light, flaky texture.

MAKES 20 PASTRIES

1 quantity chilled
Danish pastry dough
(see page 193)

Plain flour for dusting

2 medium eggs, beaten,
for brushing

100g Emmenthal, grated

For the filling

1 tbsp olive oil

1 onion, finely chopped

200g mushrooms, finely
chopped

300g Emmenthal, cut into
thin slices

Salt and black pepper

To make the filling, heat the olive oil in a frying pan, add the onion and fry gently for a few minutes, then add the mushrooms and sauté for a further 5 minutes or until they are soft. Remove from the heat, season with salt and pepper to taste and allow to cool completely.

Cut the Danish pastry dough in half. Roll out one piece of dough on a lightly floured surface to a large rectangle, about 24 x 34cm and a little less than 1cm thick.

With one long side of the pastry facing you, spread half of the cooled mushroom and onion mix over the pastry and top with half of the Emmenthal slices. Now, to roll the pastry into a tight Swiss roll, take the 2 furthest corners up over the edge of the filling and roll towards you, pulling the dough gently upwards each time you roll it to keep the roll tight. Once you have a long Swiss roll in front of you, gently roll it back and forth to seal the edges. Repeat with the second piece of dough and the rest of the filling.

Cut each roll into 10 slices and arrange on 1 or 2 baking sheet(s) lined with baking parchment or silicone paper, leaving space in between for them to expand. Put in a roomy plastic bag and leave to rise for 1 hour. Meanwhile, heat your oven to 180°C.

Brush the pastries with beaten egg and scatter some grated Emmenthal on top of each one. Bake in the oven for about 20 minutes until golden brown. Transfer the pastries to a wire rack to cool a little. Eat warm.

Chaussons aux pommes

These apple and chocolate pastries are a posh version of apple turnovers. Fruity, flaky, buttery and chocolatey, they are delicious for breakfast or brunch, or with morning coffee. You may find it difficult to resist eating them straight from the oven, but they are best left to cool for half an hour or so. A chausson, incidentally, is a Viennese pastry usually with a fruit filling that may also contain crème pâtissière, as these do.

MAKES 8–12 PASTRIES

1 quantity chilled Danish pastry dough (see page 193)

Plain flour for dusting

2 medium eggs, beaten, for brushing

For the chocolate crème pâtissière

50g good-quality dark chocolate (70–80% cocoa solids), in pieces

3 large egg yolks

50g caster sugar

1 tbsp cocoa powder

1 tbsp plain flour

150ml full-fat milk

150ml double cream

½ tbsp Calvados

½ tsp vanilla extract

For the apple purée

6 medium dessert apples

A splash of water

30g caster sugar

First make the crème pâtissière. Melt the chocolate in a bowl over hot water; set aside. Whisk the egg yolks and sugar together in a large bowl, then whisk in the cocoa and flour. In a heavy-based saucepan, bring the milk, cream and Calvados to a simmer. Slowly pour the mixture onto the egg yolks, whisking as you go. Return to the pan and cook, stirring constantly, until it has thickened and come to the boil. Remove from the heat and stir in the vanilla and melted chocolate. Cover with a disc of baking parchment to stop a skin forming and leave to cool completely.

For the apple purée, quarter, core and peel the apples, then chop fairly small. Place in a saucepan with the water and sugar and cook for about 10 minutes until softened. Blitz in a blender, then transfer to a bowl and leave to cool completely.

Roll out the Danish pastry dough on a lightly floured surface to a 6–7mm thickness and cut it into 12cm squares; you should get 8–12 pastries. Spoon 1 heaped tbsp of chocolate crème pâtissière onto the middle of each pastry square and spoon 1 heaped tbsp of the apple purée next to it. Fold the pastry into triangles and press the edges together firmly to seal.

Arrange the pastries on 1 or 2 lined baking sheet(s), spacing them well apart. Put in a roomy plastic bag and leave to rise for a couple of hours.

Heat your oven to 180°C. Pierce the top of the pastry triangles with a knife a couple of times and brush the triangles with beaten egg. Bake the pastries for 15–20 minutes until golden brown. Cool on a wire rack.

SAVOURY BRIOCHE COURONNE

Here I've adapted the more familiar sweet couronne, or crown, to make a savoury version that bursts with oozy cheese, Parma ham and fragrant basil. It's a meal in itself when served alongside a good salad and makes a stunning centrepiece on the table.

You can make the dough by hand if you prefer, but as it's a soft butter-rich brioche dough it is much easier to use a food mixer. Take your time over twisting it into shape – think about the end result and remember the filling is supposed to burst out.

SERVES 4–6

500g strong white bread flour, plus extra for dusting

10g salt

10g fast-action dried yeast

170ml tepid full-fat milk

4 medium eggs

250g unsalted butter, in small pieces, at room temperature

8–10 slices of Parma ham

3–4 balls of buffalo mozzarella, each about 125g

Small handful of basil leaves, roughly chopped

1 medium egg, beaten, for brushing

Handful of freshly grated Parmesan

Put the flour into a food mixer fitted with a dough hook and add the salt to one side of the bowl and the yeast to the other. Add the milk and eggs and mix until well combined. Add the butter, bit by bit, as you mix for a further 5 minutes. It's important to add the butter very gradually.

Tip the dough into an oiled, large plastic container or bowl and cover with an oiled lid or cling film. This dough can rise greatly and needs room to expand. Leave until at least doubled in size – at least 1 hour.

Tip the risen dough out onto a lightly floured surface. Without knocking back, roll the dough out to a rectangle, just under 1.5cm thick, with a long side facing you. Lay the Parma ham slices over the dough. Tear the mozzarella into pieces and scatter over the ham. Sprinkle the basil on top.

Roll up the dough from the long side furthest from you to enclose the filling. Roll into a sausage, 40–50cm long. Cut down the entire length of the roll, to reveal the filling. Hold the pieces firmly at each end and twist quite tightly together, moving your hands in opposite directions. Now coil the twisted dough into a circle and press the ends firmly together.

Place the crown on a lined baking tray. Put the tray inside a roomy plastic bag and leave to prove for 1–1½ hours until at least doubled in size.

Heat your oven to 200°C. Brush the top of the couronne with beaten egg and scatter with the grated Parmesan. Bake in the oven for 25 minutes, until golden brown. Leave to cool slightly and serve warm or cold.

Step photographs overleaf

Rolling out the dough to a large
rectangle, just less than 1.5cm thick.

Scattering the basil over the Parma ham
and mozzarella filling.

Rolling up the dough from the furthest
long side to enclose the filling.

Slicing the roll lengthways, splitting
it in half.

Separating the split lengths of dough.

Twisting the 2 lengths of dough together
to form a long rope.

Coiling the twisted dough and pressing
the ends together to form a crown.

Lifting the couronne onto a lined baking
tray ready for proving.

Spicy squash salad with couronne

You can make a meal out of my savoury couronne by serving it with this substantial salad. It's a delightful contrast to the soft richness of the bread, and the combination of the roasted spicy squash, salad leaves and black olives is stunning.

You can add goat's cheese if you like – it will melt deliciously into the dressing – but the salad is lovely as it is and the couronne is oozing with mozzarella.

SERVES 6

2.4kg pumpkin or butternut squash

2–3 large red chillies, deseeded and sliced

1½ tsp ground cumin

1½ tsp dried chilli flakes

80ml olive oil

150–200g pak choi

150g baby spinach leaves

Large handful of pitted black olives

300g goat's cheese (optional)

Salt and black pepper

For the dressing

5 spring onions, trimmed

3 tbsp red wine vinegar

130ml olive oil

To serve

1 savoury brioche couronne, sliced (see page 201)

Heat your oven to 200°C.

Peel and deseed the pumpkin or butternut squash and cut into 2–3cm cubes. Tip into a roasting tray and sprinkle with the sliced chillies, cumin, chilli flakes and all but 1 tbsp of the olive oil. Toss to coat and season with salt and pepper.

Roast in the oven for 30 minutes until the pumpkin or squash is lightly caramelised, turning halfway through cooking. Leave to cool slightly.

While the pumpkin is in the oven, heat the remaining 1 tbsp olive oil in a frying pan. Separate the pak choi leaves, chop roughly and add them to the pan. Wilt lightly for a minute or so, then transfer to a serving dish and allow to cool slightly.

To make the dressing, slice the spring onions on an angle. In a bowl, whisk the vinegar and olive oil together to emulsify, add the spring onions and season with salt and pepper.

Add the roasted pumpkin, spinach and olives to the pak choi. Drizzle over the dressing and toss gently. Crumble over the goat's cheese, if using. Serve the salad with the couronne.

SICILIAN LEMON AND ORANGE SWEET BREAD

This is based on the flavours of a classic Italian celebration cake called *Colomba di Pasqua,* which is similar to a panettone but shaped like a dove and sold all over Italy to celebrate Easter. Flavoured with almonds and full of citrus flavour, it's distinctive and delicious with a glass of Vin Santo or a cup of tea or coffee.

    As with many enriched doughs, this mixture is quite soft and slack and therefore easier to make in a food mixer. Buy unwaxed citrus fruit if possible, as you are using the zest.

SERVES 8–10

400g strong white bread flour, plus extra for dusting

7g salt

40g caster sugar

10g fast-action dried yeast

120ml tepid full-fat milk

4 medium eggs, at room temperature, lightly whisked

100g unsalted butter, at room temperature, plus extra for greasing

Finely grated zest of 2 lemons and 1 orange

Juice of ½ lemon

100g flaked almonds

100g mixed candied peel

100g dried cranberries

For the topping

2 medium egg whites

25g caster sugar, plus extra for sprinkling

25g ground almonds

50g flaked almonds

Put the flour in a food mixer fitted with a dough hook. Add the salt and sugar to one side of the bowl and the yeast to the other. Add the milk, eggs and butter, in small pieces. Mix on a slow speed for 3 minutes, then on a medium speed for 4 minutes, kneading to a soft, elastic dough.

Tip the dough into a bowl, cover and leave to rise for 1 hour.

Grease a 23cm round, deep springform cake tin. Mix the lemon and orange zest with the lemon juice, almonds, candied peel and cranberries. Add to the risen dough and use your hands to incorporate it well.

On a lightly floured surface, shape the dough into a ball. Put into the prepared tin and place inside a large, roomy plastic bag. Leave to prove for 3 hours, until the dough has reached the top of the tin.

Heat your oven to 200°C. Bake the sweet bread on the middle shelf of the oven for 20 minutes. Meanwhile, for the topping, in a bowl, stir the egg whites, sugar and ground almonds together to make a paste.

Take out the bread, spread the almond paste on top (some will run to the sides) and sprinkle with the flaked almonds and a little sugar. Lower the oven setting to 180°C and bake for a further 20 minutes, covering loosely with foil towards the end of cooking if it appears to be over-browning.

Leave the sweet bread to cool in the tin for 10 minutes, then release the sides of the tin. Place the bread on a wire rack to cool completely.

Limoncello trifle

This is a wonderful pudding and an excellent way to use up the Sicilian lemon and orange sweet bread. If you have time to make all the elements yourself then it is spectacular, but is also good if you buy several of them. I've given instructions for the lemon curd; you could also prepare the candied lemon zest (see below) and make your own meringues and custard. Don't rush the lemon curd or you will end up with a scramble. As for the sweet bread, buy unwaxed citrus fruit if you can.

SERVES 6–8

200g (6–8 thick slices) crustless Sicilian lemon and orange sweet bread (see page 207)

100ml limoncello liqueur

50g meringue nests

300ml carton fresh custard

300ml double cream

1 tbsp icing sugar

¼ tsp vanilla extract

For the lemon curd

2 medium eggs, plus 2 extra yolks

165g caster sugar

80g unsalted butter

Grated zest and juice of 1 lemon

To decorate

Handful of toasted flaked almonds

Candied lemon zest (see right)

To make the lemon curd, whisk the whole eggs, egg yolks and sugar together in a bowl. In a thick-bottomed pan over a very low heat, gently heat the butter, lemon zest and juice until the butter has melted. Add the egg mixture and stir constantly over the low heat until the mixture has thickened. This will take 10 minutes or longer; don't rush it. Strain the lemon curd into a bowl, cover with a disc of baking parchment to prevent a skin from forming and allow to cool. If you are not using the curd immediately then put it into a sterilised jar (see page 34) and seal.

To assemble the trifle, cut the sweet bread slices into quarters and use to line a serving bowl (about a 2 litre capacity). Drizzle the limoncello over the bread slices and spread the lemon curd on top. Break the meringue into pieces and scatter over the curd, then spoon on the custard.

In a bowl, whisk the cream with the icing sugar and vanilla extract until it hold soft peaks. Spoon the cream over the top of the trifle. Scatter over the toasted almonds and candied lemon zest. Chill until ready to serve.

Candied lemon zest

Using a zester, finely pare the zest from 2 lemons and then cut into strips. Blanch the zest in boiling water for 5 minutes, then drain and poach in sugar syrup (75g sugar dissolved in 6 tbsp water) for about 10 minutes until tender. Drain, toss in caster sugar and place on a baking tray lined with baking parchment. Set aside to dry (or place in a low oven).

SATSUMA AND DARK CHOCOLATE BRIOCHE

I associate brioche with Christmas because it's a celebratory bread in France during the festive season. Satsumas are always around at this time of the year too, so they are a natural pairing. Then the only missing ingredient for me is chocolate! I couldn't resist bringing them all together. The light richness of the brioche is lovely with a hint of citrus and niblets of dark chocolate.

This is gorgeous for breakfast or tea, eaten as it is or lightly toasted – but watch out it doesn't burn.

MAKES 1 SWEET BRIOCHE

250g strong white bread flour, plus extra for dusting

3g salt

30g caster sugar

5g fast-action dried yeast

80ml tepid full-fat milk

2 medium eggs, at room temperature

Finely grated zest of 2 satsumas or tangerines

Juice of 1 satsuma or tangerine

130g unsalted butter, at room temperature, plus extra for greasing

100g good-quality dark chocolate (70–80% cocoa solids), chopped into small pieces

For the glaze

1 medium egg, lightly beaten with a little milk

Put the flour in a food mixer fitted with a dough hook. Add the salt and sugar to one side of the bowl and the yeast to the other. Add the milk, eggs and the citrus zest and juice. Mix on a slow speed for 1 minute to combine the ingredients, then turn the speed up to medium and mix for a further 4 minutes. This will begin to form the dough.

Add the softened butter bit by bit as you mix for another 4 minutes. Now add the chocolate and mix briefly until evenly incorporated. The dough should be very soft, elastic and shiny.

Tip the brioche dough into a lightly oiled plastic container or bowl. Cover and chill overnight or for at least 5 hours to firm up.

Tip the rested dough onto a lightly floured surface. Form into a sausage and divide into 8 equal pieces, then shape each piece into a ball.

Grease a 1kg loaf tin. Place the balls in the loaf tin – 2 side by side at each end, 2 side by side in the middle and 1 in the spaces in between: a sequence of 2–1–2–1–2. Put the tin inside a roomy plastic bag and leave to prove for at least 2 hours until the dough has risen just above the rim of the tin. Meanwhile, heat your oven to 200°C.

Brush the top of the brioche with the egg glaze and bake in the oven for 25 minutes or until a skewer inserted into the centre comes out clean. Leave in the tin for 5 minutes, then remove and transfer to a wire rack to cool. Serve warm or cold.

Step photographs overleaf

Transferring the chilled brioche dough
to a floured surface, ready for shaping.

Cutting the dough in half, then into
quarters to divide into even pieces.

Cutting the dough further, into
8 equal-sized pieces.

Shaping the pieces of dough into balls
and arranging them in the loaf tin.

The shaped brioche loaf, ready
for proving.

Satsuma and chocolate brioche ice cream

Bread is a surprising but delicious base for a simple ice cream, and my satsuma and chocolate brioche makes a particularly good version. Here I caramelise the breadcrumbs with sugar and then fold them into whipped cream and eggs. A splash of Cointreau enhances the flavouring and echoes the citrus accompaniment – chilled satsumas, spiked with vodka if you like.

SERVES 6–8

100g satsuma and chocolate brioche (see page 211)

30g brown sugar

3 large eggs, separated

1 tbsp Cointreau

270ml double cream

75g icing sugar

For the chilled satsumas

6 satsumas

2 tbsp granulated sugar

150ml water

1 tsp finely grated orange zest

50ml good vodka (optional)

Preheat your grill to high. Put the brioche in a food processor and whiz briefly to medium crumbs. Mix the brown sugar with the breadcrumbs, scatter on a baking tray lined with foil and place under the grill for a few minutes to brown. Keep a close eye on them to make sure they do not burn. Set aside to cool.

Whisk the egg whites in a clean bowl until they hold stiff peaks. In a separate bowl, whisk the egg yolks with the Cointreau until thick and mousse-like. In another bowl, whisk the cream with the icing sugar until softly thickened.

Fold the egg yolk mixture into the whisked egg whites, using a metal spoon, then fold in the cream, together with the cooled crumb mixture.

Tip the mixture into a plastic container and freeze for 2 hours. Transfer the semi-frozen mixture to a bowl and beat to break up the ice crystals. Return to the container. Freeze for 2 hours or until the ice cream is firm.

To prepare the satsumas, using a serrated knife, peel the fruit, removing all the pith, then cut across into slices and place in a serving bowl. Put the sugar and water in a heavy-based pan and dissolve over a low heat, then increase the heat and boil steadily to reduce to a medium syrup (it will thicken further as it cools). Stir in the orange zest and the vodka, if using, then pour over the satsumas. Chill in the fridge.

Serve the ice cream scooped into glass bowls, with the chilled satsumas.

LARDY CAKE

Lardy cake was originally created as a special celebration cake for harvest time and other festivals. Dried fruit is dotted generously throughout the dough so you have some in every mouthful. The high fat content enriches the yeast dough and stops it from drying out as quickly as ordinary breads. My recipe uses butter as well as lard and is a bit lighter and less sweet than many commercial lardy cakes, yet still full of flavour.

MAKES 1 LARDY CAKE

450g strong white bread flour, plus extra for dusting

5g salt

14g fast-action dried yeast

75g lard

300ml water

75g unsalted butter

225g mixed dried fruit (including about 50g mixed peel)

50g soft brown sugar

Put the flour into a mixing bowl and add the salt to one side of the bowl and the yeast to the other. Mix together, then rub in 20g of the lard, using your fingers. Pour in three-quarters of the water and mix, using one hand, to form a dough. Add as much of the remaining water as you need to get a soft dough that leaves the sides of the bowl clean.

Tip the dough out onto a lightly floured surface and knead for 5–10 minutes, or until the dough is smooth. Place in a clean bowl, cover and leave to rise until doubled in size. This will take around 3–4 hours.

Tip the dough onto a lightly floured surface. Press with your fingers to flatten out to a rectangle, about 50 x 20cm. Dot a third of the remaining lard and a third of the butter over the surface. Sprinkle over a third of the sugar, then scatter over a third of the fruit. Fold the top third of the dough down, then fold the bottom third up, stretching it slightly, so the dough is folded in three and roughly square. Now give it a quarter-turn.

Roll out the dough to a rectangle, about 50 x 20cm. Layer on another third of the filling and then fold and turn as before; repeat once more.

Line and grease a 23cm square cake tin. Roll out the dough to fit inside the tin and carefully lift it in. Place in a roomy plastic bag and leave to prove for 30 minutes. Meanwhile, heat your oven to 220°C.

Bake the cake for 30–35 minutes until golden brown. Let cool slightly before removing from the tin. Cut into squares and serve warm or cold.

Step photographs overleaf

Pressing and stretching the dough out
to a rectangle, about 50 x 20cm.

Scattering a third of the sugar on top of
the dough, over the butter and lard layer.

Scattering a third of the fruit on top of
the butter, lard and sugar on the dough.

Folding the dough into three, to enclose
the filling ingredients.

Giving the dough a quarter turn and starting to roll it out again.

Rolling the dough out to a rectangle, ready to add another filling layer.

Rolling the fully layered dough to a 23cm square to fit inside the tin.

Lifting the dough into the prepared tin, ready for proving.

ACKNOWLEDGEMENTS

A huge thank you to my wife, Alexandra, for her input on this book, and to my son Joshua, for being an enthusiastic taster.

Thank you to my editors at Bloomsbury, Richard Atkinson and Natalie Hunt, for their vision and creativity. Sincere thanks to Hattie Ellis and Janet Illsley, for their excellent editorial skills, to Peter Cassidy for his genius behind the camera, to Lizzie Harris and Róisín Nield for their terrific work at the photoshoots, and to Peter Dawson and Louise Evans at Grade Design for making the book look as fantastic as it does.

Thank you to my agents Geraldine Woods and Anna Bruce. I am also grateful to Xa Shaw Stewart, Jude Drake, Amanda Shipp, Inez Munsch and Marina Asenjo.

Finally, a big thank you to the wonderful, patient crew at Love Productions, and to the BBC for making the series happen.

DIRECTORY

For equipment

Nisbets
www.nisbets.co.uk

Bakery Bits
www.bakerybits.co.uk

Lakeland
www.lakeland.co.uk

KitchenAid
www.kitchenaid.co.uk

Kenwood
www.kenwoodworld.com/uk

For flour

Doves Farm
www.dovesfarm.co.uk

Marriage's
www.marriagesmillers.co.uk

Waitrose (own brand organic)
www.waitrose.co.uk

Wright's
www.wrightsflour.co.uk

For yeast

Allinson's easy-bake yeast

Hovis fast-action bread yeast
(both widely available)